C000017440

RESISTING PO1IPHAR

Resisting Potiphar's Wife
Copyright © 2020 by Peter O. Pritchard

All rights reserved. This book or any portion thereof may not be reproduced or used in any manner whatsoever without the express written permission of the publisher, except for the use of brief quotations in a book review.

All Scripture verses are New International Version, 1984 edition, unless indicated otherwise at the point of citation. All italics and special emphasis in Scripture citations are the author's.

Printed in the United States of America

Cover Illustration by Jesse Ruffin: www.drawinguntohim.com

Cover Design by Melissa K. Thomas

Luminare Press
442 Charnelton St.
Eugene, OR 97401

www.luminarepress.com

LCCN: 2020907643
ISBN: 978-1-64388-299-4

ACKNOWLEDGMENTS

THIS BOOK IS OFFERED WITH DEEPEST THANKSGIVING, honor and worship, to my Lord and Savior Jesus Christ. Also, with heartfelt gratitude to my godly wife, June; to my supportive and loving family, and to my faithful closest friends.

And with *Special Thanks* to Emeal (E.Z.) Zwayne, President of 'Living Waters' worldwide evangelism ministry, for his very encouraging and helpful book consultation; to friends Bob and June Sturm for their generous project co-sponsorship; to very gifted illustrator Jesse Ruffin; to Patricia Marshall and the entire talented Luminare Press team. And to my devoted, caring and wise, spiritual mentor, Tom Hammon; and Young Life, the ministry through which Tom discipled me during my teen years.

This book is dedicated to all the men, young and older, Christian and seeker, who would join me in the journey for moral purity—in the freedom and victory that is ours in Christ Jesus!

FOREWORD

⁓⁓⁓

RIGHT BEFORE THE APOSTLE PAUL GIVES US THE
thrilling, incomparable nine qualities of the "fruit of the
Spirit" in Galatians 5:22, he says (for bold *comparison's* sake
as much as anything else), "The acts of the sinful nature
are obvious" (Gal. 5:19). At the top of the shameful list the
Apostle cites are the two most *"obvious"* acts of the sinful
nature: "sexual immorality" and "impurity."

That's kind of uncanny in regard to our 21st century
struggles, don't you think? In beautiful and stark contrast,
the Apostle then points out, "But the fruit of the Spirit is
love, joy, peace, patience, kindness, goodness, faithfulness,
gentleness, and self-control."

God is not against sexual pleasure—after all, he's the
one who came up with the idea. He devised sexuality
for good reasons, and made all the material and moral
provisions for it. God not only created sex for the utili-
tarian purposes of procreation (Gen. 1:27–28), but for the
purposes of providing us with the ultimate in romantic
intimacy and closeness; to bring supreme satisfaction and
thrilling enjoyment within the holy covenant and context
of heterosexual marriage. (Read Proverbs 5:18–19 and tell

me that God is against sexual fun.)

Satan, on the other hand, is the great counterfeiter. The devil is the master deceiver; in truth, the "father of lies" (John 8:44). Through pornography, for instance, he offers men *virtual* sexual satisfaction in place of what God offers us—*virtuous* sexual satisfaction.

As Christ's disciples—his precious sought, bought, and taught men of God—we must stand our ground. And where necessary, Brothers, we must *regain* and *keep* our ground, choosing *virtuous* sexual satisfaction over virtual sexual satisfaction here, now, and forever more!

We are barely into the new millennium, and it's common knowledge within the church that our times are fraught with spiritual potholes, moral land mines, and insidious cultural ambushes like never before. And each one decidedly aimed at undermining male moral sexual purity—tripping us up, Brothers—and causing failures intent on utterly *destroying* the conscience, character, marriage (if wedded), and public testimony of the man of God.

For decades, the impurity on television and in movies has promulgated its wares basically unchallenged and unabated. Now, however, the greatest innovation and single most potent implement the devil has ever had at his disposal is, undeniably, the Internet. Several factors make the Internet most useful to Satan in this regard:

1) Has *little to no censorship*

2) Is *without financial cost* (presuming one already has an Internet connection)

3) Offers *instantaneous gratification*

4) (And, perhaps its greatest advantage to our adversary, the devil) Offers a false sense of *privacy, seclusion, and secrecy*

The Internet in and of itself is, of course, *amoral*; it is merely a "medium" of communication—neither good nor bad. When critiqued solely for its technological ingenuity, it's a modern-day marvel and undeniable blessing in regard to all of the good and helpful information it can relay.

Its global content offerings and efficiencies in respect to the news, academic learning, business commerce, law enforcement, innumerable and assorted other *correspondents* and *correspondence*—not to mention the free email support it provides linking us with distant loved ones, missionaries, and our soldiers—make it of unquestionable benefit. In immeasurable ways, the Internet has truly become invaluable.

It is a tool, however, with potentially devastating implications. Just as a completely benign and unsophisticated tool of a hammer can be used to build a house or to crack a skull, the Internet has become a tool of great good, while simultaneously a tool of terribly destructive capabilities. This is particularly the case when deployed at the whims and wiles of Satan, and when so readily accessible to human hearts insubmissive to the knowledge, will, and power of God.

Matthew 16:18 indicates that the church is to be on the *offensive*—explaining that the very "gates of hell shall not prevail against it [the church]" (KJV). Much of this 31-day devotional is an unabashed, direct, frontal offensive *counterattack* to Satan's cunning exploitation of lives through his lies and lures (often via the Internet).

God created men to be emotionally, *and hormonally*, excited by the visual attractiveness of a woman's physical attributes. Right from their initial introduction to one another, Jacob was so overtaken by Rachel's outward beauty that he was willing to enter into seven years of service to her father in exchange for—*and in advance of*—her hand in marriage (see Gen. 29:17–18).

Likewise, Abraham was so aware of his wife's physical attractiveness that he convinced Sarah to lie to Pharaoh (indicating that she was Abraham's sister versus his wife); believing that, otherwise, as her spouse, Abraham's life would have been taken in order for Pharaoh to swiftly put Sarah into his spousal harem (see Gen. 12:10–13).

The ways in which our male eyes can actually bless and aid us in male/female interactions—and, in most cases, help us identify and stay enthralled with our future wives—are all part of God's good purposes. Trouble is, these male eyes of ours need some Holy Spirit (and quite deliberate on our part) *supervision*, or they frequently wander and ignite unholy and damaging imaginations.

Proverbs 27:20 describes the roving eyes of man in this alarming way: "Death and destruction are never satisfied, and neither are the eyes of man." Solomon is exposing the universal weakness of our eyes. More accurately put, he's exposing the desires of our hearts *as aided through our eyes*—having at times an *insatiable* unholy appetite, and thus, being "never satisfied." But this proverb is no mere exposé on our male propensity alone; it is a chilling warning as to what the unchecked, unbridled, lustful eyes of the male have to offer us—death and destruction.

Like-minded with the Apostle Paul's anguished lament of Romans 7:19, many of us do not do what we want to do in this regard—and inexplicably do what we *do not want to do*! This 31-day devotional is a primer intended to change that in the area of male moral sexual purity. Its aim is to "restore him gently" (Gal. 6:1), to "carry each other's burdens" (Gal. 6:2), to turn the ship around in the lives of well-intentioned, faithful men who, in some cases, literally, we must "snatch... from the fire and save them" (Jude 1:23).

In my own life, as one who's experienced unquestionable personal failure in these areas before, the Holy Spirit reminded me of Jesus's affirming words to Simon Peter shortly before Peter failed his Lord: "And when you have turned back, *strengthen your brothers*" (Luke 22:32).

I intend, with God's help, *to strengthen you,* my Brothers! And more important than that...prepare to be strengthened by God's Holy Word, the Bible. It is, after all, the only *'living'* words in all of history; the *only* words "sharper than any double-edged sword, it penetrates even to dividing soul and spirit, joints and marrow; it judges the thoughts and attitudes of the heart" (Hebrews 4:12).

Psalm 119:9 poses both predicament and solution when it says, "How can a young man keep his way pure? By living according to your word." Accordingly, we are about to examine, meditate upon, absorb, and *apply* God's holy, living, powerful Word for the victory that is ours in Christ Jesus!

The Apostle Paul admonished his dear and faithful protégé Timothy, as well as the church that Timothy was overseer of (and now *us,* the first-century church's spiritual descendants): "Flee the evil desires of youth, and pursue righteousness, faith, love and peace, along with those who call on the Lord out of a pure heart" (2 Tim. 2:22). If you're comfortable with writing in your Bible, by all means underline, highlight, or circle "along with." For let us embark on this journey *along with* one another, Brothers!

Let us *"encourage one another daily"* (Heb. 3:13), victorious to the finish line (see Acts 20:24; 2 Tim. 4:7). Let us "flee the evil desires of youth, and pursue righteousness, faith, love and peace," *TOGETHER, calling upon our God and His strength* "out of a pure heart."

May these 31 daily devotionals—an aid toward victorious purity in our lives—reinspire us and reignite the passion to rely upon the Lord Christ's deposited wisdom and strength. May they reinvigorate us to follow God and his Word the way we genuinely desire to, and *are enabled to...* and by the power of God's Spirit within us be overcomers (see Rom. 8:37). Amen!

The 1ˢᵗ of the Month

*My master has withheld nothing from me except
you, because you are his wife. How then could I
do such a wicked thing and sin against God?*

—GENESIS 39:9

Joseph, the most beloved of all Jacob's twelve sons, had
already been through so much—thrown into a dried-up
well, left to die as a result of a deep, dark bout of jealousy
by Joseph's eleven brothers. Then, he's mercifully retrieved
from the well, only to be bound and sold to a merchant
caravan that incidentally happened to come along.

From there, Joseph is transported far away from his
dearest father and cherished homeland, taken to the foreign
land of Egypt. Next, he endures the fear and humiliation of
being passed off again; this time to the highest bidder on
the infamous Egyptian slave block.

Yet, in his extremely pitiful and sad circumstance, is
Joseph bitter toward God or "Potiphar," his newly found
earthly master? Amazingly, not in the least. He is seen
maintaining respect and righteousness toward both God
and his human master.

Not long in Potiphar's service, Joseph's brawny, bur-
nished body catches the eye of Potiphar's immoral wife.
She brazenly propositions him, "Come to bed with me!"

(Gen. 39:7). Joseph immediately rebuffs her, exclaiming, "My master has withheld nothing from me except you."

How reminiscent this is to our Lord's words to Adam, "You are free to eat from *any tree* in the garden; but you must not eat from the tree of the knowledge of good and evil, for when you eat of it you will surely die" (Gen. 2:16–17).

So little does God actually restrict us from—and that which *is off-limits* is only off-limits for our own good. Psalm 84:11 perhaps says it best: "No *good thing* does he withhold from those whose walk is blameless."

Tantalizing allures of the Internet, impure images in print, film, and television—each one playing the part of Potiphar's wife—are calling out to us today, Brothers: "Come to bed with me!" And like courageous, *righteous* Joseph we can and must resist by our own inward battle cry: "God has withheld nothing from me, except you, sin! For 'no *good thing* does he withhold from those whose walk is blameless.'"

Joseph recognized that to indulge himself with Potiphar's wife (tempting as it easily might have been) was sinning first and foremost against God (see Psalm 51:4). With full knowledge of that fact, Joseph rhetorically asks, "How then could I do such a wicked thing *and sin against God?*"

Do you remember that breakthrough moment of illumination in the heart and mind of the Prodigal Son? It occurs when he's mulling over and over in his head, "Why any one of my father's hired men are better off than I am!" (see Luke 15:17).

Next, he determines that he should say to his father (if ever he sees him again), "Father, I have *sinned against heaven* and *against you*" (Luke 15:18). The Prodigal Son realized, as Joseph did, that all sin against others is actually first and foremost a sin against God.

There is another interesting aspect to Joseph's resistance, as well. Suffice that Joseph could have solely said to Potiphar's wife, "How could I do such a wicked thing and sin against God?" Yet there is a subtle, ever-important, additional little word in there we mustn't overlook: "then."

The word "then" is there in regard to Joseph's master, *Potiphar*—in regard to Potiphar's kindness toward Joseph and trust in him. Joseph is in effect saying, "How then [*in regard to my own fair treatment from Potiphar, your husband*] could I do such a wicked thing?"

For those of us who are married, there are moments of temptation when we should draw strength and inspiration from Joseph's example by employing that same key recognition. It happens by asking, "How could I sin *against her,* my wife, the woman God has me covenanted with in holy marriage?"

In truth, married or not, God's mercy and goodness toward each one of us (our very *salvation,* not to mention our daily bread and untold other blessings) immeasurably supersedes Potiphar's kind treatment toward Joseph. James 1:17 reminds us, "Every good and perfect gift is from above." Like Joseph, when tempted sexually, we too will do well to immediately ask ourselves, "How then could I do such a wicked thing and sin against God?"

The 2nd of the Month

*Sin is crouching at your door; it desires
to have you, but you must master it.*

—GENESIS 4:7

Those words of wisdom and warning were delivered, straight from the lips of God, to Cain (earth's very first murderer) *before* Cain murdered his brother Abel. If only God's words had been heeded by Cain! Sadly, instead they were immediately cast aside, disregarded, resulting in the whole shameful atrocity of Abel's killing.

Collateral damage ensued. Earth's first family, and the new society to follow, had lost a gentle faithful soul; Abel's parents, Adam and Eve, received such heartbreaking news: the unbearable pain of losing their son in this unthinkable way. And Cain, receiving his just penalty, was cursed of God and banished from God's presence—sent away to live out his days as a "restless wanderer" (Gen. 4:11–12).

Brothers, in the area of lustful temptations, pornography (including in its mildest forms of lingerie commercials and the like) is *sin that is crouching at our door!* Truly, in my own life, this sin was crouching at my door. As graphic photos and explicit scenes from TV and the Internet were becoming so prevalent in the late 1990s, I didn't go looking for porn...*porn came looking for me!*

When I moved into my new home in the summer of 1999, for instance, I might be looking for a sports or news program and unexpectedly—*unwantedly*—see a naked woman. The cable filters were not what they are today, and so *partially* scrambled images of nudity and immorality were not uncommon.

That made our televisions far from safe and benign. I remembered hearing a brother in Christ bemoan the very same issue to our pastor, in a meeting that I was attending a few years earlier. And as far as computers were concerned... similarly, it was not uncommon to be minding one's own business with pure-minded intentions while surfing the Internet, when an extremely impure image could suddenly appear. These unanticipated, unsolicited, images were called "pop-ups."

Now some twenty years later, the partially scrambled channels and impurity pop-ups no longer happen, and yet the "sin crouching at our door" is actually *more brazen.* Or it has simply adjusted to newer ways to be as sly and unexpected—and with the same abilities to trip us up whenever we are not heeding God's wise antidote: "but you must master it."

It's interesting that God used the term "crouching" to describe sin at its readiness. We almost automatically think of a crouching lion or tiger when we hear that term. A reminder of how Satan operates like a lion comes from 1 Peter 5:8: "Be self-controlled and alert. Your enemy, the devil, prowls about like a roaring lion looking for someone to devour."

Satan is on the prowl, Brothers, anxiously looking for our vulnerabilities. And to expand upon the metaphor... when he sees someone he can devour, he *crouches*, then pounces, and then "devours."

11

Far too often, and with very successful results, has the devil devoured one's righteousness, moral fortitude in this area, witness, and ministry. And obviously this form of failure undermines our marriages. And as for singles, it undermines their proper preparation for future marriage and vigilance in celibacy.

In the case of Cain's unheeded warning, sin was in the crouching position and what it seized upon was Cain's pride and jealousy, and his desire to rise above his "perceived" rival. With us, there may be all of those fallen character traits of Cain's, equally needing to ward off; but additionally, and without question, unholy sexual solicitations and associated temptations are ready to pounce at a moment's notice!

God explained to Cain that sin in its crouching position "desires to have you." In our day and age, *it desires to have us!* Put bluntly, Men, it desires *to rule over us.* Yet God said to Cain, "*You must master it.*"

The Lord would not have told Cain to "master" sin (and would not be telling us, today, through his Holy Word, the very same thing) if sin could not be mastered. *It certainly can be mastered, my Brothers!*

We will not be defeated by it and it will be mastered—*in Christ's strength and not our own:* "I can do all things through Christ who strengthens me" (Phil. 4:13 NKJV).

The 3rd of the Month

But I tell you, that anyone who looks at a woman lustfully has already committed adultery with her in his heart.

—MATTHEW 5:28

A museum's curator knows where each and every item on exhibit is located; what each item *is* exactly; and, in most cases, what each item is worth *monetarily* speaking. In far greater respect, God is the *human heart's* Curator.

The Prophet Jeremiah cried out in sheer exasperation, "The heart is deceitful above all things and beyond cure. Who can understand it?" (Jer. 17:9). Our *God* can understand it—he knows it fully. He "knows the secrets of the heart" (Ps. 44:21). The Lord Jesus, likewise, "did not need man's testimony about man, for he knew what was in a man" (John 2:25).

Jesus explains to us here that lust of the eyes for the male is, indeed, adultery; not by the letter of the law, but in spirit. God fully sees the sin, though the *woman* sinned against, in most cases, is thoroughly oblivious to its occurrence.

Seeing our sin with none of its camouflage, God is amply apprised of the fact that we have managed to flaunt and trample on three of the Ten Commandments all at once.

Right off, we have broken the 2nd Commandment: "Thou shalt not make unto thee any graven image, or any likeness of anything...Thou shalt not bow down to them nor serve them; for I the Lord thy God am a jealous God" (Ex. 20:4-5 KJV).

In the lusting over a woman, an unholy "image" has been formed in our minds. In the instances where Internet-based or other sources of pornography are viewed, that "image" is no longer in our imagination merely, but *literal*. In either case, an image—an idol—has been "served" and, in effect, been *bowed down* to!

Second, and most obvious, is that lust is a transgression of the 7th Commandment: "Thou shalt not commit adultery" (Ex. 20:14 KJV). Herein is the central point of Matthew 5:27–28; that the person who *fantasizes* impure actions with a woman has, in God's eyes, committed adultery with her—albeit "in his heart."

God is neither prude nor killjoy; it is simply that there is *unauthorized* and *unhealthy* sexuality that God intends to restrict and protect us from. God wants only what's best for us. Lust is a cheap substitute. God doesn't want us to miss out on his highest joys and highest purposes for our lives. And to that end, he demands that the precepts of his Holy Word are respected and uncompromised.

Thirdly, lust cavalierly discards the 10th Commandment: "Thou shalt not covet thy neighbor's wife" (Ex. 20:17 KJV). Any one of us who has ever lusted has coveted; we have *desired another's wife*, even if she is not married presently.

Were she *never* to marry, in fact, it is still wrong to covet that which is hers alone to offer up—her body and her sexual love. Knowing that we are prone to look for loopholes, God has left us *none* by summarizing in the

10th Commandment: "Thou shalt not covet *anything* that is thy neighbor's."

Even the unsaved and those with a secular worldview know what the term "playing with fire" means. All adulterous behavior (all the more so, full-blown adulterous affairs) were at one point instigated by mere lust and, therefore, could have been prevented had *lustful thinking* not occurred and been acted on.

Before that undeniable bold dark-red line was crossed into an adulterous affair, a hundred finer lines were ignored and crossed. The clear meaning here being, lustful rumination is not only a sin but is *playing with fire*. As the Proverb's author asks, rhetorically, on this very subject, "Can a man scoop fire into his lap without his clothes being burned?" (Prov. 6:27).

The good news in all of this is that in addition to being our heart's Curator, the Lord is truly our divine Cardiologist. He alone is able to diagnose the true spiritual healthiness of our hearts, and then is able to perform the spiritual surgical repair, as required.

He knows that regardless of what we might fake and feign in word or action, the *intentions of our heart* determine our soul's ultimate sickness or wellness. That is *how* he is able to say that he who looks upon a woman lustfully has already committed adultery with her "in his heart."

God alone can peer into the deep recesses of our heart's intentions to diagnose and correct us. If you are lost in lust, coveting what belongs to a woman alone (and if she is married, what belongs to her husband), ask God to forgive you and to heal your heart, my Brothers.

The 4th of the Month

*Then he said to them all: "If anyone would come
after me, he must deny himself and take
up his cross daily and follow me."*

—LUKE 9:23

Two remarkably different men appear in the dynamic theatre of the gospels, yet each one of them *could* have become the thirteenth disciple. The first, the previously demon-possessed man of the ten-city region called the Decapolis—now with spirits evicted and in total serenity and solidarity of mind—pleaded with Jesus to become the thirteenth disciple. Jesus refused, instead instructing, "Go home to your family and tell them how much the Lord has done for you" (Mark 5:19).

The other candidate for the tiny band of apostleship was a man who possessed every material amenity imaginable, known to us in biblical subheadings as "The Rich Young Ruler." In his case, Jesus did just the opposite—the thrilling invitation was warmly extended: "Sell everything you have and give to the poor, and you will have treasure in heaven. Then *come, follow me*" (Luke 18:22).

Dejectedly he slunk away. Mark 10:22 (KJV) explains that he "went away *grieved* for he had great possessions." He did not fully comprehend the offer. He couldn't have, or he would have known that he was spurning the greatest offer on earth! For what does it profit a man to gain the whole world, yet lose his soul? (see Matt. 16:26).

This much we do know: what he *did* comprehend was that Jesus was requiring that he *deny himself.* And that, tragically, he was unwilling to do.

In Luke 9:23, the universal siren call to Christian discipleship is sounded. The undiluted, uncompromising passion for, and pursuit of, Jesus Christ, the Lord and Savior, involves these three requisite conditions:

1) To deny oneself

2) To take up one's cross daily

3) To follow him

TO DENY ONESELF

This is the first mark of true discipleship. Are we willing to sacrifice and/or subjugate *any and all things* that impede and interfere with our obedience to Christ?

Each one of us, Brothers, has been deputized to follow the Master as he has told and taught us how. For our purposes here, are we willing to *deny ourselves* unrighteous and unauthorized sexual thoughts and experiences? If not, then we have abdicated our rights to the band and bonds of deputized disciples. Knowingly or unwittingly, we've surrendered our badge.

The Apostle Paul understood the cost of discipleship this way: "But whatever was to my profit I now consider loss for the sake of Christ. What is more, I consider *everything* a loss compared to the surpassing *greatness* of knowing

17

Christ Jesus my Lord, for whose sake I have lost all things. I consider them rubbish that I may gain Christ" (Phil. 3:7–8).

We would, each one, do well to surmise that unholy sexual circumstances and satisfactions are inconsequential to "the surpassing greatness of knowing Christ Jesus my Lord." There's no comparison at all; these kinds of sins pale by comparison and, simply put, are not in the least worth it!

TO TAKE UP ONE'S CROSS DAILY

It's fascinating to me that Jesus spoke these words *before* he went to the Cross! Who would have been surprised if Jesus had delivered this prescription for true discipleship while he unexpectedly cooked for the apostles their dawn fish breakfast (see John 21:9-10), *after* he had risen from the dead?

Surely it would have sunk in so much easier for them in that setting—that they *too* must walk in Christlike sacrificial love to the point of death—to carry their cross daily; if necessary, as Jesus did, *literally*, to a cruel and ignoble death. After all, he had earlier taught them that, "Greater love has no one than this, that he lay down his life for his friends" (John 15:13), and now Jesus had actually gone through with it!

And they had fully observed the triumphant result of that—the stunning fulfillment of Isaiah's prophesy: "Where, O death, is your victory? Where, O death, is your sting?" (1 Cor. 15:55). Jesus had brazenly triumphed over death, and his disciples could, as easily, have anticipated that death would neither conquer nor confine them either. In light of that, this second requirement to true discipleship (to take up their cross daily) would make perfect sense.

But of course, the *post-resurrection* campfire breakfast cooked up by the risen Lord is not when and where these words were spoken. Since this was told to them *prior* to the cross of Calvary, what were they to make of such language? To daily take up thy cross?

They would have perceived it solely in view of the common occurrence of the condemned, each one carrying their crosses to execution! To see it from that vantage point raises the bar still higher to the call of sacrificial, unwavering, slave-like devotion. If we, each one of us, are prepared and willing *to carry our cross daily*, one would think we would be willing to resist in the face of sexual temptations... even terribly fierce ones.

TO FOLLOW HIM

The Rich Young Ruler was no doubt reeling from the requirements of forsaking all, so much so that he barely even noticed that Jesus had said to come follow him. That little addendum meant everything, and he missed it! By following Jesus, he would have been giving up nothing of value whatsoever. As Psalm 73:25 explains, *"earth has nothing I desire besides you [God]."*

The Apostle Peter was feeling both prideful and put out all at once when he complained, "'We have left everything to follow you!' 'I tell you the truth,' Jesus replied, 'no one who has left home or brothers or sisters or mother or father or children or fields for me and the gospel will fail to receive a hundred times as much in this present age (homes, brothers, sisters, mothers, children and fields—and with them, persecutions) and in the age to come, eternal life'" (Mark 10:28–30).

To follow Jesus is all at once protection, provision, and purpose. Why there is no better invitation in all of life! Shepherds lead sheep, and we are the sheep of his pasture (see Psalm 100:3). Because the Lord is my shepherd, *I have everything I need* (Psalm 23:1, Living Bible translation).

When we are sexually unfulfilled, we need to turn the Shepherd of our souls for strength and guidance. "It is God who arms me with strength and makes my way perfect" (Psalm 18:32). He "makes my way perfect." That doesn't mean free of problems; that means perfect as in the right and chosen pathway for me—in order to fulfill his "perfect" plan for my life, and in order that God will be most glorified.

In all venues of life, we must remain a "disciple" of Jesus Christ, and no less in areas of our sexuality. When tempted with sexual impurity, we must *deny ourselves*, remembering our Lord has denied himself immeasurably *more* on our behalves.

When tempted with sexual impurity, we must *take up our cross daily*. And unlike those doomed and despairing, trudging to their death via a cruel ancient mode of execution, this is not for us a *one-time* event; but as Christ says, something that must occur *daily*—a lifestyle of day-by-day obedience and subjection to Christ's will over our own. And because Christ knows and wants what's best for us, this is not tragic, but triumphant!

Most of all, Brothers, when tempted with sexual impurity, we must *follow him*, not our unrestrained impulses and appetites, but truly follow and obey the One most worthy of following!

The 5th of the Month

The Lord disciplines those he loves, as a
father the son he delights in.

—PROVERBS 3:12

Several years ago, I unintentionally awakened on a Saturday morning at something like 5 a.m. I felt too tired to get up for the day and yet was too alert to simply go back to sleep.

In that condition, and hoping not to awaken my wife, I reached for the remote and turned on the TV on its stand just past the foot of the bed. TCM, the Turner Classic Movies channel, was the channel that appeared when the TV came on. (My wife had been watching that channel when the TV was last on during the prior evening).

Before I changed the channel in search of the intended ESPN or a world news channel of interest, I observed a woman in a nightgown on a bed facing someone off camera. In an instant, the Holy Spirit quickened my soul that I *must urgently turn the channel at once!*

In my partial wakefulness, yet with fully alert curiosity and momentary disobedience, I lingered on the channel a bit longer. Sure enough, the nightgown swiftly came off and a gentleman off camera, hence coming into view, proceeded to join the actress in bed.

I turned the channel before witnessing the rest of the sex scene, but, sadly, it was too late…I had not averted and avoided the very thing the Holy Spirit had warned me of. I had sinned and now (as our Scripture verse today points out) my sin received a loving, but stern, discipline from the Lord. Truly, my guilty conscience and sullied soul felt just awful. I promptly asked God's forgiveness. It was granted to me—of course it was, as his Word promises this (see 1 John 1:9)—but the *heavy hand of the Lord* upon me for what I had done didn't dissipate.

As soon as the daylight hours reached a more reasonable time, I called a close friend and brother in Christ that I knew I could confess to and repent before; someone that I knew I would receive prayer and compassion from without judgment. I got his voicemail and, without leaving details, asked that he call me back as soon as possible.

The rest of the weekend, the heavy hand of the Lord— *his loving discipline*—only marginally lifted. My friend and I never spoke until after the weekend. When we did, he told me that when he listened to my voicemail message Saturday morning, the Holy Spirit told him not to call me back!

Dear Brothers, your experiences of discipline from the Lord have been, and will continue to be, entirely different from mine…but discipline, nonetheless, it will be! God loves us too much not to discipline us until Christ is formed in us.

God has actually designed us *to receive benefit* from feeling bad over our sin. The Apostle Paul went so far at one point as to direct the believers *not to associate* with a Christian brother that "does not obey our instruction…*that he may feel ashamed.*" Not to treat him "as an enemy," Paul explains, but caring enough to "warn him as a brother" (2 Thess. 3:14–15).

No discipline is pleasant, even when its outcomes have lasting value. "All discipline for the moment seems not to be joyful, but sorrowful; yet to those who have been trained by it, afterwards it yields the peaceful fruit of righteousness" (Heb. 12:11 NASB). Being trained in righteousness is a good thing, but I don't want to experience the unpleasant aspects to the training any more than I absolutely need to!

During that weekend, the ancient biblical message of Psalm 32:4–5 was lived out and experienced in its most contemporary and timeless application in my life: "For day and night *your hand was heavy upon me*; my strength was sapped as in the heat of summer. Then I acknowledged my sin to you, and did not cover up my iniquity. I said, 'I will confess my transgressions to the Lord', and you forgave the guilt of my sin."

The 6th of the Month

For you have spent enough time in the past doing what pagans choose to do—living in debauchery, lust, drunkenness, orgies, carousing and detestable idolatry... What benefit did you reap at that time from the things you are now ashamed of?

—1ST PETER 4:3; ROMANS 6:21

Sometimes when I am tempted, I think of these verses and doing so provides immediate strength. It produces a tactical impediment to otherwise tumbling forward on a collision course toward the desired sin.

When these passages come to mind, there is really only one alternative to their stopping me in my tracks; it is to in effect argue with the Bible's wisdom here—making the defense that I have *not spent enough time* doing what the pagans choose to do! How ludicrous and brazenly rebellious that sounds. Doesn't it?

King David lamented, "For I know my transgressions and my sin is always before me" (Psalm 51:3). Each one of us could make the same admission. We largely know *how* we have sinned and *how much* we have sinned.

The Apostle Paul poses his question ("What benefit did you reap at that time from the things you are now ashamed of?") because he confidently knows what the answer is.

His question is rhetorical. And in the hindsight of 20/20 perspective, he's confident they feel a certain remorse and ughh over such actions.

Paul knows that God's church in Rome that he's addressing *will know what the answer is.* And surely the Holy Spirit knows that future believers (you and me considering this today, my Brothers) will know the answer...how those things we are now ashamed of were of *no benefit* whatsoever. Are we, therefore, now to deceive ourselves into believing that somehow those things *were good* for us after all? Are we to delude ourselves into believing that *this time* delving into some kind of sexual misbehavior *will be different*? That truly we have *not spent enough time* doing such things?

Can we actually mean to say, with a straight face, to the Holy Spirit, "Please allow me to add one more transgression to the list. Surely God will forgive me, and *this time* it will accomplish the lasting satisfaction in my soul that has eluded me every single other time—when it solely resulted in shame, heartache, disappointment, and dismay." Any such internal debate with the Divine would be comical were it not so outrageous.

James, the Lord's earthly half-brother, had it so right, explaining, "when lust hath conceived, it bringeth forth sin: and sin, when it is finished, *bringeth forth death*" (James 1:15 KJV). And how similar James's insight is to this passage from the Psalms: "He who is pregnant with evil, and conceives trouble, *gives birth to disillusionment*" (Psalm 7:14).

Along with that, our selected passage in Romans 6:21 concludes with these searing words: "Those things result in death." That is what giving in to the Internet sirens of sin, or any other lustful temptation, has to offer us—disillusionment and death! I do not want disillusionment and death. I know you don't either, Brothers.

Let us pray: Father, help us this day and each day to remember that we have spent far too much time in the past doing what the pagans do. And to what benefit? None whatsoever! Help us, Lord, to remember the end trail of sin, leading to disillusionment and death, that awaits those who disregard your truth and power. Rather, help us to choose and receive your holiness, truth and power, contentment and life! In Christ's name, Amen!

The 7th of the Month

*No temptation has seized you except what is
common to man. And God is faithful; he will not
let you be tempted beyond what you can bear.
But when you are tempted, he will also provide a
way out so that you can stand up under it.*

—1 COR. 10:13

To take God at his word here is to believe that God wants
us to be wholly victorious over temptation every time—
not to be abject failures, ever falling into sin, controlled by
sin, with little difference now versus the unredeemed man
of our prior lives.

God wants us to be changed, empowered—*VICTORI-
OUS*. And in this passage God is *promising to assist us* in
such a way that we will always win...Did you hear that?...
I said, *ALWAYS WIN...provided we want it bad enough* to
follow the signposts to God's deliverance from trouble. To
look for, to find, to accept and employ *God's help* at those
moments means when temptations come, we will be able
to "stand up under it" and be victorious every single time.

The Apostle Paul instructed the slaves of ancient times
who had become Christians, "If you can gain your freedom,
do so" (1 Cor. 7:21). In order for that Christian slave to take
advantage of his freedom, however, he had to *recognize* it

when it was offered. At each and every point of temptation, we are offered our freedom. The Scripture text we
are examining here confidently reassures us that our God
"*will—provide—a—way—out!*"

The question is, do we believe this? Will we recognize the "way out?" Do we even *pause* and slow down at
moments of temptation...*in order to pray*...in order to
discover and recognize the way out that God has provided?

There is a bodily pang that supersedes the physical
pang for sexual satisfaction—that is the pang of hunger and
thirst. Jesus felt it intensely: an unrelenting ache for relief
from hunger after his forty days of fasting. Many will say
after several days of fasting that the pangs of hunger go
away, but others will attest just as assuredly that they never
entirely subside.

Have you ever fasted from food (entirely, not eating a
single morsel) for twenty, thirty, or forty days? I have not,
but I have an extremely close and amazing friend who has
done so on a number of occasions. Each time he has attested
that his hunger pangs for food never fully subsided.

That is what is corroborated here regarding Jesus's experience, when after forty days of fasting, Luke 4:2 describes
that "he was hungry." This is why Satan did not appear with
bags of gold or with a compliant, compromising woman in
alluring apparel. Jesus's bodily ache was for none of those
things. It was plain and simple hunger, and that was exactly
what Satan intended to exploit in challenging Jesus to turn
stones into luscious, *mouthwatering bread*.

With uncanny consistency to our Corinthians study
today, God had earlier said in Deuteronomy 30:11, "What
I am commanding you today *is not too difficult for you.*"
Jesus knew this principle, and so he held strong.

Did you know that technically speaking Jesus did not have to hold out? He could have said, "Devil, you really need a better timepiece. You're, foolishly, *one single twenty-four-hour day* too late! My forty-day fast has just been completed, and I have more than earned what you are suggesting."

But even though Jesus was anxious to satisfy his body's justifiable demands, he was not willing to allow Satan to exalt himself over God, and to usurp God's will for his Son. So, Jesus drew upon God's strength within (*the strength God is offering each one of us today*) to remain faithful. He remembered and recited, in faith, to the devil, "Man does not live on bread alone, but on every word that comes from the mouth of God" (Matt. 4:4)

When we are tempted, we are inclined to say, "This is too powerful for me!" But in truth, we are misinformed at those times. Jesus said in Matthew 22:29, "You are in error because you do not know the Scriptures or the power of God."

To say, "This is too powerful for me" is be misinformed of *the Scriptures* and misinformed regarding *the power of God*. For God has promised "*he will not let you be tempted beyond what you can bear*." God has promised to provide us with "*a way out*" so we "*can stand up under it*" in every single ungodly circumstance.

In order to escape, however, we must believe our Holy text today…that "God is faithful" … and perceive the way out that he has provided…and then take it!

The 8th of the Month

*Submit yourselves, then, to God. Resist the devil,
and he will flee from you.*

—JAMES 4:7

We've all heard since the infancy of our individual Christian belief that "our struggle is not against flesh and blood, but against the rulers, against the authorities, against the powers of this dark world and against the spiritual forces of evil in the heavenly realms" (Eph. 6:12). And it's absolutely true. The gauntlet has been thrown down. In terms of spiritual warfare, the gladiator games to the death have commenced!

Happily, we know the final outcome...Satan loses, we win, yay! (See Rev. 20:10, Rev. 21:3–4.) Even so, until that final hour in which the devil and his dark angels are completely vanquished, we daily war in the *spiritual* realm, and with far from insignificant consequences in the *material* realm.

Sadly, most believers are not very skilled in the hand-to-hand combat the demonic players incite and engage us in. Perhaps we shall solve a very crucial missing puzzle piece to this common predicament here and now...

I am convinced we are very often too quick to jump into the spiritual melee—believe it or not, *too ambitious and too quick* to "resist the devil." Our error at such times comes from going to Step #2 while never fully satisfying the prerequisite Step #1.

The most important piece of instruction in James 4:7 is the part that is most often overlooked (and usually never quoted) when this passage and spiritual principle is employed. That is the *first part* of the verse: "Submit yourselves, then, to God."

So many times, we have resisted the devil with great earnest (perhaps even great faith), and he seems to not even flinch in the face of our resistance. At those times, we must ask God, "In what ways am I *not submitting to you, LORD?*"

The devil and his demons are powerless and unsurprisingly cowardly in any showdown with God (see James 2:19, Matt. 8:29). God will do his part; and the devil and his rodent servant spirits *will flee from us,* as surely as this passage promises. The devil flees, however, only when he sees that it is a man *submissive to God* who is standing up to him. Reason being, at such times we are standing firm and resisting the devil *in God's strength,* not in our own.

It is only at those times that the Archangel Michael's tactic of Jude 1:9 (saying, "the Lord rebuke you!") may be employed by us mere humans; and at minimum, that we would be able to pray to God with total confidence: "deliver us from the evil one" (Matt. 6:13).

Prepare yourself for this at least partial explanation to your *unsuccessful* spiritual warfare…if you are resisting God, the devil has no reason to cease from attacking you. This bears repeating…*If—you—are—resisting—God—the—devil—has—no—reason—to—cease—from—attacking—you!*

However, if you are not resisting God, but are yielding to God's plan and provision of help, the devil is then powerless. For in truth, it suddenly becomes the Lord at those times of your spiritual warfare with the demonic *who is fighting the battle for you*! And God can never lose, Hallelujah!

Actually, James is not introducing all that new of an idea in terms of how God wants us to cooperate with his deliverance in our lives. Speaking through the voice of his prophet Asaph in Psalm 81:13–14, God explained, "If my people would but listen to me, if Israel would follow my ways, how quickly would I subdue their enemies and turn my hand against their foes!"

In what ways might you be resisting God today? Perhaps you know fully well. Perhaps you have been slow to obey something in your relationship with God…and it may not even be in the area of sexual purity. It may be something related to your prayer life, your financial giving, your treatment of your wife or kids, or regarding some other person or matter of importance in your life.

That said, if you think there may be some area of your life that is not fully yielded to God, but aren't clear on what that is, God can personally, and precisely, reveal to you the answer to this…and he is wanting to do so.

But do you *truly want the answer*? God will show you when he knows you're serious about getting to the crux of your resistance, and are ready and willing to fully yield to him.

The Psalmist, King David, asks in Psalm 19:12, "Who can discern his errors?" The question itself is replete with the answer…*no one fully knows*. Not without God's help, that's for sure. Accordingly, David prays next: "Forgive my hidden faults. Keep your servant also from willful sins."

David recognizes that there is so much we don't see, that we don't know, do not fully comprehend about the ways in which we offend the Lord. So, David petitions God, "Forgive my *hidden faults*" (those sins that are hidden to himself but certainly not hidden to God).

And then to make sure all of his bases are covered, David addresses the sins that he is *well aware of* that he's committing, praying, "Keep your servant also from *willful* sins."

If God will forgive us for our *hidden* sins, and keep us from the willful, *deliberate* ones, we shall become more and more like him—that is, *holy*! The prayer continues on that in *either* case, hidden or willful, "may they not rule over me."

When these prayers are answered, we are in submission to God. When we are in submission to God, we may resist the devil, and the devil will surely flee from us!

Let us pray: Father God, we have offended you so many times and in so many ways. Many of them are hidden to us, none of them hidden to you. We are deficient in fully discerning our errors; although many of them, we must concede, are in fact *willful*. We earnestly desire to be holy and pure before you in the area of sexual purity. Please forgive and root out our hidden faults. Above all, keep us from the willful ones. And let neither hidden nor willful sins rule over us. When the devil attacks, may he come up against lives in such submission to you, Father God, that the tempter must flee from us as we resist him! In Christ's name, Amen.

The 9ᵗʰ of the Month
Morning

*For the grace of God that brings salvation has
appeared to all men. It teaches us to say "No"
to ungodliness, and worldly passions, and
to live self-controlled, upright and
godly lives in this present age.*

—TITUS 2:11–12

The very elegant "First Lady" of the 1980s, Nancy Reagan, is credited with creating the slogan and positive anti-drug campaign aimed at kids, "Just Say No," during her husband's presidency. Its goal was to provide kids the impetus, and a tool, in order to reject dangerous, illegal, recreational drug use.

Nancy Reagan's antidrug-use campaign was modestly effective and no doubt produced some tangible good, yet here in Titus is something so much more potent than any slogan and government advertising blitz. We're talking about "the grace of God" (verse 11). It is that *grace* which, according to God's Word, "teaches us to say 'No' to ungodliness and worldly passions."

It is sad, even shocking to some degree, that any one of us Christian men would ever need support in this way—

in the area of lust or pornography. One might think that anything as primal, unseemly, and ungodly would hold no appeal to the *regenerated* man in Christ. The truth, however, is that if all worldly passions were entirely extinguished at the point of salvation, we would be immortal and all admonitions in Scripture on how to best live on earth would have no point to them.

We are being taught how to say "'No' to ungodliness and worldly passions" because God's Word is conceding here that some measure of weakness in temptation stubbornly hangs on. Elsewhere, the Apostle Paul admonished God's church, "do not let sin reign in your mortal body so that you obey its evil desires" (Rom. 6:12). Paul would not have to give this directive if the "evil desires" had completely ceased to exist. Unfortunately, this side of heaven they can be very persistent.

Still, we can take heart that God will not ask anything of us that he has not prepared and equipped us to success-fully accomplish in our lives. When his Word says, "do not let sin reign in your mortal body so that you obey its evil desires," it means we don't have to! We don't have to allow sin to reign in our mortal bodies. We don't have to obey sin's evil desires. We can *"Just Say No!"*

God transcends time. He knows the end from the beginning and everything in between. He has not been caught off-guard by the onslaught of immorality on our TVs and in our movie theatres, and which is so readily accessible on our computers and smart phones today. Some-times we act as if we're thinking, "If only God had known how bad it was going to get!"

He knew, he knows, and he has the solution for it—the solution is *Himself*. He is here for us, he is within us; and

35

he will guide and empower us to be overcomers—here and now, TODAY!

God is promising that his grace, the grace that "brings salvation" and that has *"appeared to all men,"* will teach us how to do the things we need to in order to achieve victory in areas of sexual purity—teaching us "to say 'No' to ungodliness, and worldly passions, and to live self-controlled, upright and godly lives in this present age."

How do we know this still works? We need look no further than that little phrase at the end of our passage: "in this present age." God put that in there because he knew that until Christ returns, Christians shall read his Word and in turn apply this to each believer's *own* specific times… our own specific temptations…our own specific needs…*in our own present age!*

The 9th of the Month

Evening

Through the fear of the Lord, a man avoids evil.
—PROVERBS 16:6

My four children are adults now. They grew up knowing, *thankfully*, that their earthly father mightily loved them! They never feared me in the way anyone of us fears persons or things capable of bringing harm or evil upon them; they knew me too well for that. They knew that wasn't *possibly* going to come their way from one who loved them so very deeply.

But they, nonetheless, feared *the consequences* of disregarding my directives; they feared the consequences I might bring upon them for, plainly put, getting in trouble…for things like speaking disrespectfully to their mother, or to me, to one another, teachers, to *anyone* really—or for not turning the TV off when it was time, not coming home on time, telling a lie, or not fulfilling their age-appropriate responsibilities.

And for such wrongs, there were going to be consequences worthy of their avoiding. Discipline in our home usually meant a restriction (from going to a sleepover, staying up late, etc.) that they would surely feel the sting of disappointment over missing out on.

Of course, all of the unpleasant consequences were meted out by me (and their mother) in fervent love, and all done in the hope of, and in the shaping of, their greatest character and best future. When the kids feared the painful consequences, they behaved better, or...regrettably...tried harder and smarter not to get caught!

God's Proverb 16:6 here (and other places in his Holy Word) explain that when we truly fear God—and not in the sense of *being afraid of him* but in fearful reverence and awe of him—we will adhere to his good pathways more closely. Fearing the *loving but stern* consequences God will bring upon his children (*for our own good* and as result of disobedience and folly) is a very wise and fruit-bearing motivator.

Truthfully, the Bible has an awful lot to say on the subject of fearing God. Proverbs 9:10, Psalm 112:1, and Psalm 25:12 are just a small sampling of this. I think if we are honest with ourselves it makes good sense. Here's why:

The Apostle Paul had no doubt in his mind that the Roman church would know perfectly well what it means to fear 'human,' civil authorities. So, he took a few moments to strongly urge the church to, at all times, stay on the smart side of the strong arm of the law, stating, "For rulers hold no terror for those who do right, but for those who do wrong" (Romans 13:3).

He continues from there with the most logical of questions and advice: "Do you want to be free from fear of the one in authority? *Then do what is right* and he will commend you" (Rom. 13:3). Finally, Paul concludes with this strongest of warnings, "But if you do wrong, *be afraid*, for he does not bear the sword for nothing" (Rom. 13:4).

Like our Roman kinsmen of many centuries ago, twenty-first century Christians are fully up to speed on the benefits of obeying the civil laws, as well as the risks of disregarding them...we get it. As my wife once astutely pointed out, even the serial killer (strange as it may seem) is no doubt stopping for red traffic lights on his way to do the killings!

So why are we less apt to fully comprehend the benefits of obeying—and the risks of flaunting—*God's* laws? Psalm 19:11 reads, "By them [the ordinances of the Lord] is your servant warned; in keeping them there is great reward."

Are we now to view God's laws as less important, less unchanging, and less correct and laudable than the human laws we readily toe the line with? And is God less concerned, less vigilant, than the human civil law enforcers to see that *His* laws are respected and upheld?

The good news is that as we absorb this truth and respect God as one to be properly feared, it actually keeps us from running afoul. It promotes discipline and purity in us (the very thing we're seeking) in order to please God and have the best lives possible. "We have all had human fathers who disciplined us and we respected them for it. *How much more* should we submit to the Father of our spirits and live!" (Heb. 12:9).

The 10th of the Month

As iron sharpens iron,
so one man sharpens another.

—PROVERBS 27:17

One of the more disappointing changes I have observed
in some of the most recent Bible translations (in ver-
sions you can easily find) is an alteration to this Proverb
27:17 verse. In some Bibles it will now read, "As iron sharpens iron, one person sharpens another person."

I do not for one minute believe that those newest translations capture the inspired Word-of-God message the
Lord intends to get across in this passage. Without question, a godly woman can edify and encourage, admonish
and advise ("sharpen" if you like) another woman...and,
yes, also do the same, for his clear benefit, to a man. And
certainly, a man can (at times and with proper decorum)
represent and provide these same helpful things to a
woman.

But wise King Solomon says, very deliberately, in this
passage, *"As iron sharpens iron"* a *"man sharpens another."*
Iron sharpening iron in biblical times (tooling for the
benefit of farming or for war) was blacksmithing *done by
a man.* With thorough knowledge of the metallurgy of
his day, King Solomon had seen iron sharpening iron and

was keenly aware that iron sharpens iron with great force, determination, and precision—and that it produces sparks!

In nearly all cases, none of us prefers for any male to be as tough with a woman as we can be with one another. It begins when we playfully rumble on the carpet or ground together as very young boys, and from there progresses into fist fights and contact sports such as football, wrestling, and hockey.

Then, spiritually speaking, it culminates with a hardened, direct, "tough love" approach to helping one another grow in Christ-likeness, accomplished *through how we speak with one another*—brother to brother, *man to man.*

As Proverbs 27:9 so aptly puts it, "the pleasantness of one's friend springs from his earnest counsel." This is accomplished by "speaking the truth in love" in our unique male-to-male way (Eph. 4:15).

And to what end? According to the very same Ephesians verse…in order that we, each one of us, would *"become in every respect the mature body of him who is the head, that is, Christ"* (Eph. 4:15 NASB).

Over the years, I have had men of God (starting way back when I was a youthful teen, very young in the Lord) who have sharpened me "as iron sharpens iron." To this day, thankfully, I have a few men in my life—*very transparent and direct with one another*—that sharpen one another's walk in Christ, as iron sharpens iron.

We have been willing to tell one another difficult-to-hear hard truths when it is in the other's best interests. The very same chapter of Proverbs gives us a clear example of this in verses 5–6 when it says, "Better is open rebuke than hidden love. Wounds from a friend can be trusted."

The only kind of brother in Christ that can accomplish

this in fruit-bearing, life-giving fashion, however, is that brother who *has earned one's trust*. And that special bond of trust develops through these two qualities: love and confidentiality.

The first of those requirements is *love*—Holy Spirit-directed love. This is the kind of person whose brotherly, rock-solid, love is so undeniable and dependable that he qualifies for the description, "there is a friend that sticks closer than a brother" (Proverbs 18:24).

The second requirement is *confidentiality*, and that aspect to the relationship is solely borne out of trust. Jesus said to the Twelve Disciples, *minus Judas*, "I no longer call you servants, because a servant does not know his master's business. Instead, I have called you *friends*, for everything that I learned from my Father *I have made known to you*" (John 15:15). Jesus is plainly telling his disciples that he trusts them!

The remaining eleven had earned Jesus's trust. "A trustworthy man," Proverbs 11:13 tells us, "keeps a secret." In actuality, Jesus was explaining here that he could be confidential with them. He also, most importantly, *felt their love*. Perhaps in no greater way had Jesus indicated this than when he told them, "You are those who have stood by me in my trials" (Luke 22:28).

Brothers, do you have a man…or better yet, *a few men…* in your life who have earned your trust? Who have had your back? *Who have stood by you in your trials? And who earnestly love you and can keep a secret?*

When you know that these *brothers* love you and can be spoken to with total confidentiality, then you have someone you can regularly turn to for support in the area of sexual purity.

Brothers, let's face it, we are *BOMBARDED* on a nearly daily basis with things (on television, our tech devices, and our *real-life surroundings*) that the enemy strategically places in our pathways to make us stumble in this area.

But as iron sharpens iron, there is a trusted, tried and true (and at appropriate times *hardened*) friend that you can turn to who will lift you up in prayer! And this is to great benefit, for the "effectual fervent prayer of a righteous man availeth much" (James 5:16 KJV). Also, when helpful and necessary, he will ask some relevant questions and regularly *keep you accountable* in the area of sexual purity.

I implore you, *please*, with God's help, pray for and discover such a man for your life if you do not yet have one. God will welcome—*answer and reward*—such a request, and he will provide you with this man or men.

As we turn to such a brother—and also provide such comfort and support to him in return, where desired—we are strengthened. *We are sharpened*, my Brothers. To God be the glory!

The 11th of the Month

Be still, and know that I am God;
I will be exalted among the nations.
I will be exalted in the earth.

—PSALM 46:10

Sometimes it seems like the hardest thing on earth to do
is to just be still: to be patient, quiet, trusting, compliant.
To take no action whatsoever…to do nothing.

In truth, this biblical admonition is not exactly about
doing nothing, but to do *nothing more than* to simply be
still before the Lord—which means to be solely attentive to
God and his voice; rather than the noisy clatter all around
us (externally), and all the noisier inner tantrums of the
flesh (internally).

Even though it goes against our nature to be still, Christians must have come to the conclusion we're good at it,
because this verse is quoted a lot. Virtually never, however,
are the verses before it and immediately subsequent to it
quoted at the same time.

That is unfortunate, for it is in its broader context
within the Psalm that we can fully absorb its aid and application; its serene efficacy regarding our *daily battles*—most
pertinent to us here, Brothers, in the battle for, and pursuit
of, personal purity.

The preceding and subsequent verses read, beginning in verse 9: "He makes wars cease to the ends of the earth; he breaks the bow and shatters the spear, he burns the shields with fire." And verse 11 reads: "The LORD Almighty is with us; the God of Jacob is our fortress."

Have you ever felt your struggle for purity is no minor struggle but an all-out *WAR* in your mind and soul? Then remember: He makes *wars cease* to the ends of the earth, and he says, "Be still and know that I am God."

Have you ever felt like the bows, spears, and shields of Satan and the world are all aimed at you personally, with the one goal being your moral failure? In fact, dedicated to your entire spiritual destruction? Then remember: He *breaks* the bow and *shatters* the spear; he *burns* the shields with fire, and he says, "Be still and know that I am God."

Have you ever felt *totally alone* in your struggle? Then remember: The LORD Almighty *is with us*, and that he says, "Be still and know that I am God."

Have you ever wished there were someplace to *escape* to? Someplace where you could go and hide to feel safe and secure, and wholly protected? A place where the attacks could not even penetrate? A place which could only be described as a *fortress*? Then remember: "the God of Jacob is *our fortress.*" And he calls out to us within the fortress, "Be still and know that I am God."

In the area of sexual purity, to be still and know (to remember and rely upon) that *God is God* becomes a very valuable resource—a tried and true, reliable *biblical* strategy for deliverance.

There have been times when I have been under attack in some area of temptation and have been merely still before the Lord. And when I have done so, the attack has receded.

And then if I have remained still just a little longer, it has retreated and then vanished from whence it came.

Let God be exalted among the nations! Let God be exalted in the earth! He whispers to us even now, "Be still and know that I am God."

The 12th of the Month

The widow who lives for pleasure is
dead even while she lives.

—1 TIMOTHY 5:6

This 31-day devotional is aimed at *men*, not widows, so why explore a verse such as this? Because at its core is a principle we men can learn an awful lot from.

Much of chapter 5 of 1st Timothy is devoted to rules for the care and eligibility of "widows," but within this little verse is a big principle that applies to anyone at all; and that principle is this: *the one who lives for pleasure is dead while he lives.*

This "death" Paul speaks of is not literal, yet the Apostle has employed that word in order to make his strongest point possible…and it's a very sobering thought. When we live for pleasure—*when we make choices to accommodate the desire for temporal and temporary sensual satisfaction over obeying God*—we are dead, spiritually nonresponsive, disconnected from the life of God.

We've all heard unbelievers describe Christians as "nothing more than a bunch of hypocrites." That is largely an unfair and overreaching generalization. Many times, in fact, it is an accusation levied not to challenge Christians to exhibit lives that more accurately exemplify the Lord, but is more likely spewed to deflect the spotlight off of their own darkened souls and conscience-burdened actions.

Nevertheless, sadly we must concede, there are many times when the charge is well-deserved. In those instances, there is no one more concerned and more vigilant to exfoliate the forgery—more interested in evoking true change in the person—*than the Lord*. Among other choice words, Jesus boldly exposed such religious fakes as "whitewashed tombs," saying to their very faces, "you hypocrites!" (Matt. 23:27).

Today, as then, there are people who are extremely *outwardly* religious with little to no inward authenticity—persons who have gotten "Churchianity" down pat. They know precisely when to say "Praise the Lord!" and be deemed very spiritual. They are well skilled in crinkling their brow and looking most solemn when they say, "I'll pray for you." Meanwhile (like the "whitewashed tombs" of Jesus's stinging rebuke) their lives are anything but pleasing to God!

Most likely they know which church events to show up for, versus the ones during which their absence will likely go unnoticed (or at minimum their absence is least likely to be viewed unfavorably). All the while they appear "beautiful on the outside," according to Jesus, "but on the inside are full of dead men's bones and everything unclean" (Matt. 23:27). And all because they are most interested in securing "praise from men more than praise from God" (John 12:43).

God forbid, Brothers, that *any one of us* would look just grand on the outside—saying and doing all the right things at church and in front of our Christian friends—while on the inside we are *dead*; or may as well be because, in truth, we are living for pleasure. This is exactly what happens when we slowly, but steadily, give in to the titillating lies and lures of sexual temptation Satan strategically places before us on a nearly daily basis.

Christ has proclaimed, "I am the vine; you are the branches. If a man remains in me and I in him, he will bear much fruit; apart from me you can do nothing. If anyone does not remain in me, he is like a branch that is thrown away and withers; such branches are picked up, thrown into the fire and burned" (John 15:5–6).

When we give into Internet porn, sex and nudity in movies, or otherwise-induced impure thoughts, we are both "without fruit and uprooted" from the Lord—what Jude 1:12 calls *twice dead.* We are voluntarily cutting ourselves off from the true Vine, Jesus Christ; thus, *incapable* of bearing spiritual fruit, and being cut off from God (the source of our life-sustaining nourishment), we spiritually wither and die.

May we never "live for pleasure," my Brothers, but instead always live for the Lord!

The 13th of the Month

*If your right eye causes you to sin, gouge it out
and throw it away. It is better for you to lose
one part of your body than for your whole
body to be thrown into hell.*

—MATTHEW 5:29

Jesus presents this unsettling mental picture immediately
after his rather startling pronouncement that he who
"looks lustfully" upon a woman has "committed adultery
with her in his heart." Jesus is trying his best to make sure
the seriousness of this sin is neither overlooked nor in the
least minimized. He is additionally giving a prescription
for its avoidance.

Is it the human eye and its optic nerve, with 137 million
photoreceptors (called *rods* and *cones*), that is offending and
sinning when lust is occurring? I don't think so. And if it
were the case, then Jesus would be solving the problem once
and for all (by saying, "Get rid of that organ of the body!");
though simultaneously creating a host of new problems, as
his servants stumble through their remaining days on earth
in physical chaotic blindness.

No, in fact, ironically by using such a gory and implau-
sible suggestion, Jesus is highlighting the fact that it is *not
the eye* that is sinning. It is you. It is me. It is *the heart* that

50

is directing those eyes. Jesus had only moments before made it perfectly clear that the person who has sinned in this way is committing adultery "*in—his—heart.*" Those were Jesus's exact words.

Now that we've placed the discussion in its vital context, how must we respond? We must *redirect the heart,* and to do that we must not minimize this issue. Lust is too ferocious, too unwieldy, and (at first) untamable to be taken lightly. We have to approach this thing as Jesus is imploring us to do so—as if our very eternal destiny depended on it!

Jesus is saying, in effect: Let's be logical about this. As horrific and excruciating as it would be to gouge one's eyes out—awful and inexplicable to *deliberately* blind oneself—it would be *far worse* to go merrily to hell with both eyes in perfect working order!

And, of course, Jesus is right. Given the choice between that extreme pain and loss here and now, yet be granted the reward of eternal life...*or*...to be spared that irrevocable impairment on earth but receive eternal damnation and the terrors of hell, any thinking male would instantly choose the eye-gouging (like Samson faced, see Judg. 16:21). Blessed be the Lord, that we are not *literally* faced with those two choices!

Nevertheless, Brothers, are we willing to treat the sin of lust that seriously? Are we willing to employ *extreme measures* (as Jesus is more than implying) in order to maintain righteous and pure thoughts toward women?

Are we willing to spend a bit of money (if necessary and helpful to the fight) in order to have an adequate Internet filter on our computers? Are we willing to have a Christian brother set it up without our knowing its password, to prevent its discretionary disabling? Are we, at the very least, willing to expose our level of temptations and failures with our pastors or trusted Christian brothers for prayer support, strategy, and accountability? You get the idea.

Gouging out our eyes, so to speak, plainly means taking actions that are severe, probably representing a legitimate cost of some kind (at minimum *to our pride*) in order to honor God, and putting a red-alert priority on personal vigilance in this area.

To act otherwise is to respond in an unconcerned and unserious manner toward something God is not at all unconcerned and unserious about. If he were so unconcerned, he would not have given us the dramatic and gruesome example Jesus gives us in Matthew 5:29!

The 14th of the Month

I will set before my eyes no vile thing.

—PSALM 101:3

Perhaps God in his own divine foresight allowed the inventors of TV to call it the "television *set*" with this scriptural principle in mind. Think about it: "I will *set* before my eyes no vile thing." It's an interesting coincidence of sorts.

Certainly, the television set has been a great purveyor of "vile" things for many years. From its prolific vulgar language to scenes of nudity and sexual situations, to its endless dirty jokes, and assorted anti-God and immoral plot lines. And I'm just thinking about the standard fare of the major networks; this is to say nothing of the far less restricted immorality smorgasbord on pay-for-view and main fare cable movies.

The trouble isn't TV, however. The trouble isn't movies, the trouble isn't Hollywood big business, and the trouble isn't the Internet either—the trouble is *us*! The trouble is the inclinations of our hearts—the inclination of hearts, that is, when uninclined and unresponsive toward God.

All of the above industries and mediums only sell what we, the public, buy—*what we want*. It's that basic. They would clean up their act in a New York minute if our entertainment appetites were transformed to the point that we no longer desired their garbage, and no longer watched it when it's offered. Like the Prodigal Son in Luke 15:16, the typical entertainment consumer is, spiritually speaking, so far from home that he longs to fill his belly with what the pigs are eating.

Truth is, if the average entertainment consumer didn't have such *appetites*, the advertisers underwriting these mediums would be forced to spend their dollars elsewhere in support of cleaner programming because their current target audiences (who are buying their products) wouldn't be there anymore.

For now, sadly, they have no such inclination or incentive. It's quite the opposite when, as the Bible makes plain, "the wicked freely strut about when *what is vile is honored* among men" (Psalm 12:8).

In the 101st Psalm, God is putting the burden of a smut-free zone in our homes squarely on our *own* shoulders. In declaring, "*I will* set before my eyes no vile thing," the Psalmist (King David) is taking personal responsibility.

And he goes even further to reinforce this in the verses just prior and subsequent to it. Psalm 101:2 reads, "*I will* be careful to lead a blameless life—when will you come to me? *I will* walk in my house with blameless heart." And then verse 4 continues, "Men of perverse heart shall be far from me; *I will* have nothing to do with evil."

It takes constant effort to be pure before the Lord. This 31-day devotional is about taking on an ardent work ethic about this. It should be encouraging to us that King David is modeling this for us. He says, "*I will be careful* to lead a blameless life." And it doesn't happen automatically, Brothers.

David is committing his own willpower and determination to make it so, yet simultaneously (and in such precious fashion) is acknowledging his utter *dependence upon God*—calling out for God's help ("when will you come to me?"), without whom no success would be possible. On that basis, David is dedicating himself to this righteous course: "*I will walk* in my house with blameless heart."

Would it be fair to say that people writing, producing, and performing in perverse ways for the purpose of our supposed *entertainment* could be characterized as "men of perverse heart"? If so, then we need to rethink whether we should be so happily "near" to them, *embracing* their products—*paying* for their products. Or like David, do we want them far away from us? He emphatically decries, "Men of perverse heart shall be far from me."

Then he goes further to say, "I will have nothing to do with evil!" This is the fourth instance in the Psalm, by the way, that King David is taking *personal responsibility* for his righteous environment and righteous choices.

Let us pray: Father God, please forgive us for we have not been blameless in terms of vile things we have knowingly set before our eyes or, at the very least, not averted our eyes from. Give us the determination of King David to walk blameless in our own homes. Keep purveyors of perversity far from us, and help us to have nothing to do with evil. Last of all (*first of all really*) Lord, *we need more of you.* We echo David's entreaty: *When will you come to us?* In Christ's name, Amen.

The 15th of the Month

*Watch and pray so that you will
not fall into temptation.*

—MATTHEW 26:41

Leave it to our Lord Jesus to so succinctly distill the remedy for temptation down to these two simple and most important things: first, *WATCH*, so that you will not fall into temptation; and secondly, *PRAY*, so that you will not fall into temptation.

Watch for what? For the obvious temptations that come our way, and for the *not so obvious* ones.

Remember Satan, personified in the form of the serpent, was the "craftiest" of all God's creatures (see Gen. 3:1). The King James Bible casts a slightly different, but perhaps more enlightening, nuance to the serpent's predominant characteristic in the events of the garden. It calls him the most "subtle" (Gen. 3:1). And with great consistency to that thought, the Apostle Paul says that Satan is prone to disguise himself as an "angel of light" in his attempts to sway us by the most camouflaged, discreet, and unanticipated means (2 Cor. 11:14).

Temptation is continually coming at us. And then after it has come, *watch*, for it's coming back again! Jesus was not tempted by one of Satan's underlings—some foot soldier of the demon world—but was tempted by Satan himself, standing there in living color. And after Jesus gave Satan his thorough dressing down and utterly demolished his sly demonic tactics, the devil "left him *until an opportune time*" (Luke 4:13).

Satan was down but not out. He was leaving with his ego bruised, head drooped, and pointy tail between his legs, but what the Word confirms here in Luke 4:13 is that the devil, nonetheless, would surely strike again. God directly promised the devil, to his face, that ultimately Jesus Christ (the "seed" of Eve) would "crush [his] head" (Gen. 3:15), but this was not that hour; and so, Satan would regroup to look and to linger for his next best opportunity.

The devil and his demons are that way with us as well. Saints Matthew and Paul do not call Satan "the tempter" (Matt. 4:3; 1 Thess. 3:5) without good reason...*the devil tempts!* And when he is successfully repudiated by our faith and the Word of God, he has not (this side of heaven) ever resigned himself to leaving us alone entirely, but has only been removed for the time being—and then only to regroup until another "opportune time."

Jesus is imploring us, therefore, to stand guard. Don't fall asleep at your watch post. If you do, the results may be disastrous.

"Your enemy, the devil, prowls around like a roaring lion looking for someone to devour" (1 Pet. 5:8). He wants to devour our faith, and unfortunately one of the quickest, fastest-acting ways he can cut us down to size is with inciting LUST—particularly well aided by pornographic imagery and, at times, merely *sensuous* imagery (think the *Sports Illustrated* swimsuit issue and half the television commercials).

The Apostle Paul said, "we are not unaware of his schemes" (2 Cor. 2:11). Can we say the same thing? I fear not, Brothers. It's as if we have been lured into the lion's den thinking there is a cuddly cozy kitten in there instead of a hungry, hostile man-eater.

Watch! Don't be naïve nor reckless about the things that draw you into temptation. Are you strong enough to go to the beach on a hot summer day? Only you and God know the answer to that. Are you wise and strong enough to flip to another station when a Victoria's Secret commercial or the Dallas Cowboys cheerleaders come on?

Are you prepared to hit the "skip button" the moment the sex scene is starting its set up (not actually begun) in the Netflix movie or on your DVD player? And let's be honest, Men, in most cases the films give us sufficient advance notice prior to the actual indecency appearing before us.

Are you disciplined enough to gaze down at the floor or to go get some popcorn during scenes with sex or nudity at the theatre? The examples could go on, but surely you get the idea.

I, for one, don't choose to take the chance of lacking self-control at such moments. Since the film industry's own rating system includes (in every single television or banner ad) exactly *why* they are rated PG-13 or rated R, I don't go to the movies (nor watch Netflix, etc.) that warn of nudity and sex scenes.

And then Jesus says, "Pray," so that you will not fall into temptation. It is the other half of Jesus's instruction here and very reminiscent of Jesus's model prayer: "And lead us not into temptation" (Matt. 6:13, Luke 11:4) from what's commonly called "The Lord's Prayer."

The Lord never tempts us (James 1:13); in fact, just the opposite is true. He is the overarching guiding force and protector over the lives of his believers.

It isn't surprising, therefore, that Jesus would beckon us into prayers that we *not* be "led" into temptation and that we *not* "fall" into temptation. That we would consistently pray to God that he would navigate us *away* from persons, places, powers, and circumstances which might exploit areas of weakness in us.

These prayers are not only wise, but necessary! Jesus defined the constant risks, explaining, "The spirit is willing, but the body is weak" (Matthew 26:41).

And when Jesus says, "pray, so that you will not fall into temptation," he is *not* merely saying, "Pray *these precise words* and you will be safe." He is teaching us this in the broader context of the other things that God has to say to us about an effectual prayer life.

He is saying, pray for this ("that you would not fall") with *faith* (Mark 11:24, James 1:6). Pray for this as much as possible at the *earliest* start in your day (Mark 1:35). Pray for this when you can steal away from the urgent demands of each day's responsibilities for *longer periods* (Luke 6:12); and pray for this with *regularity* (Acts 3:1).

Pray for this with *persistence* (Luke 11:5–10); pray for this *fervently* (James 5:16 KJV). Pray, *not* with selfish motives but with the prime motive of *glorifying God*, and with *humility* (James 4:3, James 4:6). Pray with an attitude of *thanksgiving* (Phil. 4:6); and at least some of the time, pray with one, two, or more prayer partners (Matt. 18:19, Acts 12:12).

If you are on a treadmill going nowhere in terms of improving in areas of sexual purity—in your *thinking and behavior*—please consider these guidelines for effectual alertness and prayer concerning temptation. Then ask yourself, "Am I *watching* and *praying*?"

The 16th of the Month

Elijah went before the people and said,
"How long will you waver between two opinions?
If the Lord is God, follow him; but if Baal is God,
follow him." But the people said nothing.

—1 KINGS 18:21

Baal is the most prominent of all Old Testament idols, and most likely for this simple reason: he was the "god of rain." In the Middle-Eastern world (much of it very arid), and at that time in history of premodern irrigation ingenuity, dependence on rain was something akin to dependence on air—nonnegotiable to survival.

Thus, in a society uninformed about, or uninterested in, worshiping the *true* Lord (Yahweh), their devising a god *who is responsible for the rain*—who dispenses rain upon his own whims and appeasement—is not in the least surprising.

Regardless of how unremarkable that may be, the Prophet Elijah is not amused nor slightly tolerant of their vain, pointless, and *apostate* religion. If rain is what is needed, then only the true Lord, Maker of heaven and earth, is to be consulted and petitioned! That is why Elijah challenges his kindred Israelites (*ones who should know better*), "How long will you waver between two opinions?"

Elijah simplifies things for them saying, "If the Lord is God, follow him; but if Baal is God, follow him." The rest of the story is really worth reading (and rereading), for Elijah goes further than his arresting challenge to them. He demonstrates in very courageous, miraculous, and *undeniable*, fashion just which One true God is real and worthy of their undivided worship and devotion.

When we are drawn into the world of lust or porn, even its mildest forms, we need to say to ourselves as Christian men, "How long will you waver between two opinions? If "Eros" (the "false god" of *erotic* pleasures) is God, *follow him*; but if the Lord is God, *follow him!*"

Satan, and our own resilient traces of fallen man within, would seduce us at moments of temptation into believing that sexual pleasure is as vital as air or water. It is not! So let's use our heads for a moment, Brothers; take Elijah's advice, and get off the fence. Which one is God? Stop wavering between two opinions and choose.

Jesus said similarly, "No one can serve two masters. Either he will hate the one and love the other, or he will be devoted to the one and despise the other" (Matt. 6:24). James 1:8 teaches us, as well, that the double-minded man is unstable in everything he does.

One of the final things Jesus says in the entire Bible is, "I know your deeds, that you are neither cold nor hot. I wish you were either one or the other!" (Rev. 3:15). Like Elijah before him, Jesus dares us to make up our minds. And if we will not, he continues, "So because you are lukewarm, neither hot nor cold, I am about to spit you out of my mouth" (Rev. 3:16).

Like those lukewarm believers Jesus rebukes in the Book of Revelation, our passage of study today records the *astounding* indifference: "But the people said nothing." Elijah desperately wanted to see them get off the fence, to choose between their "two opinions." They were neither hot nor cold, however, and therefore "said nothing." May it never be true of us, Men!

Let us pray: Lord Jesus, we choose you and you alone. We love you, and we want no part of the false god "Eros," worldly sexual arousals, and all things Satan and our own stubborn human tendencies would deceive us into holding onto. We want no part in believing *that impurity is beneficial at any level.* Please forgive us for all the times we have been of two opinions in this matter. Shore us up to be *inferno red-hot* for you—steadfast in our hearts and single-minded to follow you and you alone. In your name we pray, Amen.

The 17th of the Month

When I saw that they were not acting in line with the truth of the gospel, I said to Peter in front of them all, "You are a Jew, yet you live like a Gentile and not like a Jew. How is it, then, that you force Gentiles to follow Jewish customs?

—GALATIANS 2:14

Naturally each one of us Christian men genuinely want our life to be a vibrant living testimony to the truth and vitality of the gospel. We are disciples of Christ, after all, and our Lord has commanded, "Go into all the world and preach the good news to all creation" (Mark 16:15).

We want to see others come to faith in Christ, *as we did.* That said, when any single aspect of our lives invalidates or undermines the truth and power of the gospel, we severely diminish the effectiveness of our witness.

Paul cuts straight to the heart when he sees that Peter is "not acting in line with the truth of the gospel." No matter how well we disguise it, no matter how hard we pretend the sin issue isn't present in our lives, we know (and God surely knows) when we are not acting in line with the truth of the gospel. Our witness is inauthentic at those times—and, consequently, will produce little to no spiritual fruit-bearing.

Paul is in effect saying to Peter, "You can't have it both ways! You can't live as if you're not a Jew, all the while imploring others to embrace the Jewish religion." The same goes for us Christians. We can't be passionately advocating others to come to saving faith in Christ, to turn from sin, to turn from living for self toward living for God, when it's actually *not working for us!*

When there's that kind of discrepancy in our lives, we reduce our once vibrant, authentic, testimony to sullen silence. Or the other alternative is we speak out as fervently as ever, simultaneously *cringing inside* from the blubbering hypocrisy ringing out in our own heads.

Christ wants us to be his witnesses. Acts 1:8 shares the immensely confidence-building news that we shall "receive power" for the task. The Lord Jesus has left us the Holy Spirit in order to accomplish this. Jesus, himself, is no longer on earth in the flesh; yet mysteriously he is! He is here in us, in his church, by his spirit living within us: "Christ *in you*, the hope of glory" (Col. 1:27; also see Matt. 28:20).

And because of this fantastic fact, there is no need for timidity: "For God hath not given us the spirit of fear; but of power, and of love, and of a sound mind" (2 Tim. 1:7 KJV). The very next verse, 2 Timothy 1:8, tells of a tremendous aspect, purpose, and benefit believers shall have with the spirit of power and love and a sound mind living within us. "So [in light of this fact] do not be ashamed *to testify* about our Lord."

If we are not right with the Lord, if we are living some kind of phony double-life, we will be ashamed (and rightly so) to testify to the Lord in our lives—the very thing 2 Timothy 1:8 is urging us to do. Thankfully, this same spirit that accounts for our *boldness* is also within us demonstrating power, love, and a sound mind in order to accomplish and preserve our *righteous* witness.

Jesus said, "You are the salt of the earth. But if salt loses its saltiness, how can it be made salty again? It is no longer good for anything, except to be thrown out and trampled by men" (Matt. 5:13). We are to *season* the world with the hope and truth of the gospel and, like salt, create a *thirst* in our hearers for the One, solely, who is able to quench the vacant, parched soul and spirit.

When we participate in areas of impurity*, we are the ones who are spiritually dry. We have lost our saltiness, and how may we regain it? Only by repentance, by God's grace and God's mercy. Otherwise, our testimonies are "thrown out" (Matt. 5:13). In a court of law our testimonies would be viewed as *inadmissible*—not enough true factual evidence to convict—and we have set ourselves up for having our witness (like savorless salt) "trampled on."

Instead of a silenced witness, Brothers (or worse yet, a *hypocritical* witness), we need our purity restored, our hearts reignited, our faith renewed, and a righteous—*factually correct*—witness "in line with the truth of the gospel." For this we pray, Heavenly Father. In Christ's name, Amen.

*And it doesn't take a lot. We don't have to be addicted to porn. Even our chronic mild accommodations to the lusts of the flesh can disrupt and diminish God's will and work in our lives: "A little yeast works through the whole batch of dough" (Gal. 5:9; also see Mark 4:19).

The 18ᵗʰ of the Month

His divine power has given us everything we need
for life and godliness through our knowledge of
him who called us by his own glory and goodness.

—2 PETER 1:3

It is so easy to feel incomplete, dissatisfied in life—about our finances, our kids, our career, our sex life, our marriage or singlehood; our church, our health, our looks, our in-laws, our sense of accomplishment (especially after about age 45 or 50); our golf score, our make and model of car, blah blah blah. Satan's mischief, and our own mixed potion of self-pride and self-pity, can make us inwardly pretty discontented folks.

When that is our predominant individual disposition in life, we can be very miserable inside and, at minimum, vulnerable to the need for some added *excitement*; and far too often, receptive to a little *unholy* excitement for our lives.

Our Scripture passage today is the antidote for this. The Lord's "divine power has given us *everything we need* for life and godliness." How reminiscent it is to the beloved through-out-the-generations 23ʳᵈ Psalm and its opening stanza: "The Lord is my shepherd; I shall not want." How can we be lacking and unfulfilled when he has provided for everything we need *for LIFE*? That pretty much covers ev-er-y-thi-ing!

I know it takes faith to always absorb this truth, and I am far from always mature in this, Brothers, but then as the Apostles once said to our Lord Christ, "Increase our faith!" (Luke 17:5). Or as the father, seeking relief for his demonized child, exclaimed to our Lord, "I do believe; help me overcome my unbelief!" (Mark 9:24).

Day by day we must work on believing and absorbing this truth, which will immeasurably help us in our steadfastness and pursuit of personal purity. If God's divine power has given us everything we need for life, then we should be content, full, satisfied—and that means no longer restless and open to adding "unholy excitement" to our mundane lives.

According to this passage, "his divine power" is what *enables us* to lead the kinds of lives God wants for us—*the lives we genuinely desire*—reflecting personal godliness. His divine power (not a power from within our human spirits or emanating from any pop psychology, latest books, fad teachers, or any other external source, but from God alone) has given us "everything we need *for life and godliness.*"

When a demon whispers in the night, "You can't do it," or we murmur to our very own souls, "I can't do it," we are misinformed. We can do it! We can do it by *his divine power,* and by something else this passage teaches..."*through our knowledge of him* who called us by his own glory and goodness."

How is your "knowledge of him" who's called you? Perhaps you are still an infant (spiritually speaking) when you should be mature by now. God forbid the scathing indictment of Hebrews 5:12 fits any one of us when it says, "Though by this time you ought to be teachers, you need someone to teach you the elementary truths of God's Word all over again. You need milk, not solid food!"

In that verse and the subsequent verses 13-14, the writer of Hebrews is visibly agitated. It is because he sees a need for *retraining* in "righteousness," and in the ability to "distinguish good from evil" (the very thing we are striving for in this 31-day devotional). Something he believes they should have long before this become mature in. Something he considers "*elementary* truths."

Perhaps you haven't read God's Word (the four Gospels in particular) lately, or nearly that much at all in your Christian life and have only a superficial, introductory knowledge of *him who's called you.*

Get more! Dive into the Gospels anew! You will be appropriating his divine power for greater godliness in your life as you *gain more knowledge of Jesus.* It's promised here and, in doing so, you will gain understanding and greater belief that he has given us "everything we need for life and godliness." And that includes in areas of our sexuality, my Brothers.

The 19ᵗʰ of the Month

But among you there must not be even a hint
of sexual immorality, or any kind of impurity...
Have nothing to do with the fruitless deeds
of darkness, but rather expose them.

—EPHESIANS 5:3 AND 5:11

Whﾑen you think of the church on a nationwide basis, and some of its most prominent leaders, do you think of an institution and body of people that have been free of *"even a hint* of sexual immorality or any kind of impurity?" When you think of the church you presently attend, and the ones you've attended in the past (including close Christian friends of yours), do you think of a church and fellowship of believers that have been free of even a hint of sexual immorality?

When you think of your own life (particularly the life that only you and God see), do you think of a man who's blameless of even a hint of sexual immorality? Have we, as Christ's church body that thrives today, utterly failed? And, if so, is the Apostle's admonition here to be free of "even a hint" of such darkness within us truly possible?

The Apostle Paul wrote nearly one-fourth of the divinely-inspired New Testament. God performed mighty miracles through him. He evangelized much of the Ancient

Mediterranean world. He endured floggings and persecution like few others before or since, ultimately being killed for his faith. He is someone to esteem and admire, to be inspired by, and to learn a great deal from.

But he was, through it all, *still a man like you and me.* And while he clearly is inspirational to us in issues of abstinence and sexual purity matters, he evidently had a temper and impatience about certain persons; and in ways I'm not sure the Lord is asking anyone to emulate.

For instance, go and review Galatians 5:12, Titus 1:12, or 2 Timothy 4:14 the next time you're short or unkind with someone you care about; you just may feel a bit better about yourself. You'll still need to go and apologize, but you may feel less like a *total failure* in your Christianity at that moment.

I say this to remind us that Paul was a man—a regular red-blooded Y chromosome male, and men (as you know) have a hormonal tempest going on much of the time that is barely under control, let alone entirely dominated. Nonetheless, Paul, by the power of the Holy Spirit, understood that these impulses *can* be tamed, and *must* be tamed if we are going to emulate (in fact *represent*) Jesus Christ accurately and effectively to the world.

First off, we must continually remind ourselves that these deeds (according to our text here) are *F-R-U-I-T-LESS!* That means of *no benefit* to ourselves or anyone else.

Jesus Christ has called us to bear fruit (the complete opposite of "fruitless" by the way); and not only that, but he intends for us to produce *lasting* fruit (see John 15:16). We cannot produce his fruit, and have lasting fruit to God's glory, if we are still playing around with fruitless sexual titillations of one kind or another...Make sense?

Our text today doesn't candy coat it: we are to have *"nothing to do with the fruitless deeds of darkness."* How can there be so much sexual sin in the church—in supposedly God-fearing persons—while we are having "nothing to do" with such things? When we consistently fail in this area, it is tragic. It's as if we don't take the admonitions of Scripture—the true marks of Christ's Lordship and our discipleship—very seriously.

We are not only to be personally and collectively blameless concerning sexual sins, we are called to "expose them" (Eph. 5:11). And here's a very important thing about that added requirement...it doesn't mean embarrassing people.

By exposing them, Paul is not talking about *talking* about those embroiled in them. If that were what Paul means by *exposing* these sins, he wouldn't follow up those instructions with immediately *contradicting* himself, saying, "For it is shameful *even to mention* what the disobedient do in secret" (Eph. 5:12).

What he means by exposing them is exposing the "deeds" (without pointing fingers) within our fellowships—and, most of all, in our own hearts and minds—for what they are: *fruitless deeds of darkness.* Paul is urgently coaxing us out of the darkness (where things are hidden, unexposed) back to where we belong, where everything is *exposed* under the light of Christ: "You were once darkness, but now you are light in the Lord. Live as children of light" (Eph. 5:8).

Certainly, we would do well at all times, my Brothers, to remind ourselves of that. But it is only wise to particularly remind ourselves of this truth (with *heightened awareness*) when experiencing some measure of sexual temptation—to speak to our own souls, at such times, with this *precise* Scriptural clarity and wisdom Paul has spoken of here:

"You were once darkness, but now you are light in the Lord." And to speak to our soul with great authority and biblical confidence, boldly declaring, "Live as a child of light." And finally, at such times of temptation, to ask ourselves, "Is this thought or action that I am contemplating representing darkness or light?"

The 20th of the Month

*Although they claimed to be wise, they became
fools, and exchanged the glory of the immortal
God for images made to look like mortal man...
They exchanged the truth of God for a lie, and
worshiped and served created things rather than
the Creator—who is forever praised. Amen.*

—ROMANS 1:22-23 AND 1:25

There are few things more foolish than irrevocably
exchanging one's precious birthright for a bowl of lentil
stew, as Esau did (see Gen. 25:29–34). Yet when a Christian
man is lulled and lured into the snare of impure images, he
is doing something arguably worse—exchanging "the glory
of the immortal God *for images*" and bargaining away "the
truth of God *for a lie*."

In the case of Esau, one is voluntarily sacrificing a
temporal privilege (a birthright) and "human glory," so to
speak; in the case of our beholding sexual imagery, we are
handing over something far more precious—the "truth of
God" and the "glory of the immortal God." Not to mention,
it is also trifling with one's *spiritual* birthright.

It's kind of fascinating when we consider this: it has
been nearly two thousand years since the Bible's unmiti-
gated condemnation of idol worship involving "images,"

and now, again in our current times, the moral stumbling block of "images" has remarkable modern-day relevancy!

The ancients would carve or hammer out images in timber and stone, bronze, silver, and gold, all in the hope that in paying it some kind of reverence, the satisfied idol would materially improve their lives. Tragically, even the people of Israel—*God's people*—were often coaxed into this demonic, worthless enterprise.

After only a few centuries of the Christian church's advance, and the steady progression of societal and technological developments, archaic idolatry of bowing down to blocks of wood, stone, or metal greatly diminished; the practices now, if they even still exist in remote regions, are imperceptible to modern society.

Isn't it ironic then that with the advent of printing, then photography, then motion pictures, then television, and now the Internet, the human spirit has *devolved* to the point that the dire biblical warnings involving *images* has once again taken on such relevancy for modern man?

The Psalmist of Psalms 115:4–9 exposed the folly and futility of turning to images for support this way: "But their idols are silver and gold, made by the hands of men. They have mouths but cannot speak, eyes, but they cannot see; ears but they cannot hear, noses but they cannot smell; they have hands but they cannot feel, feet but they cannot walk; nor can they utter a sound with their throats. Those who make them will be like them, and so will all who trust in them. O house of Israel, trust in the LORD—he is their help and shield."

Today's pornographic images, likewise, have no actual life in them—no breath, no sight, no hearing, no touch, no sense of smell. And *neither shall we* if we indulge in them!

The warning is unambiguous: *Those who trust in them will be like them* (Psalm 115:8). To be like them is to be unable to speak, to see, to hear, to feel. It is *to be without senses*—to be *senseless*. Brothers, obviously we do not want to be senseless, without our senses—at best, to become "fools" (Rom. 1:22–23) by receiving such comfort from images.

None of us would *ever* want to exchange the "glory of the immortal God *for images*" fashioned to look like a mortal [woman]. We don't want to "exchange the truth of God *for a lie*." And yet, *we are being led to do that very thing* whenever we are led to believe that there is satisfaction, fulfillment, and enjoyment (without disastrous consequence) in indulging in impure images.

The Psalm 115 passage just examined concludes with this impassioned plea: "O house of Israel, trust in the LORD—he is their help and shield." And I will make mine: O Brothers of the house of Jesus, *trust in the LORD—he is our help and shield!*

The 21st of the Month

*If I had cherished sin in my heart, the Lord
would not have listened; but God has surely
listened and heard my voice in prayer.*

—PSALM 66:18–19

What is the Christian life if prayer is eliminated? Or if while still being prayerful, it is rendered meaningless, ineffectual, pointless?

Prayer is our most vital and indispensable implement for connecting with our Maker. Praise and worship are our highest expression of love *to* God...Bible instruction our highest enlightenment *from* God...service and love to others our highest expression *of* God...but the benefit to all of these hinges on prayer—our highest intimacy and communication *with God.*

Humble, sincere, consistent prayer is how we enter into social, personal, intimate dialogue and communion with the Creator of the entire Cosmos. It is how we have intimate and personal communication with the Creator of all matter and space and time—with the very Savior of our souls.

Is such intimacy and connection with the Divine too amazing and thrilling to be true...that this is truly *even possible?... yet, it is true, Brothers!* Righteous Job referred to "God's intimate friendship" in Job 29:4. That is worth our strenuously striving after and experiencing—that each one of us would enjoy *intimate friendship with God*!

"Come near to God and he will come near to you" (James 4:8); "by prayer and petition, with thanksgiving, present your requests to God" (Phil. 4:6); "And I will do whatever you ask in my name, so that the Son may bring glory to the Father" (John 14:13); "Before a word is on my tongue you know it completely, O LORD...Such knowledge is *too wonderful for me*, too lofty for me to attain" (Psalm 139:4 and 139:6).

As Christian men we must do anything and everything in our power to ensure that nothing dilutes our prayers. Romans 3:23 teaches us that "all have sinned and fall short of the glory of God" (also see Prov. 20:9, Eccles. 7:20).

Since we all fall short (repeatedly), then the key word in today's devotion is "cherished." Is there any sin of impurity, Brothers, you are holding onto...in truth, that you are *cherishing*? Peer into your hearts for a moment and take closer inventory of what God sees in there. Then ask yourselves, is there any area of impurity you are reluctant to let go of?

Is there any flash drive or old DVD with scenes of impurity you are unwilling to toss out?... any unrighteous magazines stashed away in your truck or garage or secret drawer? Is there any *mental fantasy* of some woman (in your past, in your everyday life, or perhaps some celebrity) you keep going back to in your mind?

Is there anything saved on your computer hard drive that beckons you into sin periodically? Only you and God know it's there*. You know it should go; you know it's done your soul not an ounce of good, but you've not been ready or able to get rid of it.

*"Nothing in all creation is hidden from God's sight. Everything is uncovered and laid bare before the eyes of him to whom we must give account" (Heb. 4:13).

These are examples of sins that have become "cherished" in your heart. Today is the day with the forgiveness, power, hope, and help of the Holy Spirit to *stop cherishing* it! Today is the day to stop going back to it; in fact, to *permanently,* once and for all, remove and destroy it if it exists in any form.

Proverbs 28:9 says, "If anyone turns a deaf ear to the law, even his prayers are detestable." We can't go a stone's throw further in our Christian walk, Men, if our prayers are detestable to God.

Jesus died for us so that the barrier between us and our Holy God is now removed. He died so that we would daily enter God's presence with "confidence," set free from sin, "to receive mercy," and that God would "help us in our time of need"…all in response to our daily prayers (see Heb. 4:16).

If we are married and holding onto any area of impurity, the Word of God informs us we have *especially* hindered our prayers: "Husbands, in the same way be considerate as you live with your wives, and treat them with respect…*so that nothing will hinder your prayers*" (1 Pet. 3:7).

To my married Brothers: How can we treat our wives "with respect" if we are sinning against them (whether they know it or not) in areas of sexual impurity? And if we are disrespecting them in this regard, God's Word is assuring us that our prayers are hindered.

Let us pray: Father God, we know that if our prayers are hindered, detestable, or worst of all *unlistened to,* we have broken trust with you and have broken off priceless fellowship with you. Please forgive us for those times; restore us to righteousness and strength. And for those of us who are married, keep us always respectful to our wives. Married or single, may we never cherish sin; that we could always, like the Psalmist in our lesson, be able to say, "but God *has surely listened* and heard my voice in prayer." In Christ's name, Amen.

The 22ⁿᵈ of the Month

*The eye is the lamp of the body. If your eyes are
good, your whole body will be full of light. But if
your eyes are bad, your whole body will be full
of darkness. If then the light within you is
darkness, how great is that darkness!*

—MATTHEW 6:22–23

To think of the eyes as "bad" at first blush reading here
is to think of eyesight that is damaged, dimmed, or
shuttered in such a way as to reduce visibility to utter
blindness. That's a very unpleasant thought. After all, Jesus,
himself, once pointed out, "If a blind man leads a blind man,
both will fall into a pit" (Matt. 15:14).

And to that point, just about everyone knows that
if a person's eyes are bad enough to result in blindness,
or even greatly reduced vision, then life is extremely
difficult and restricted. This is of tragic and terrible
consequence.

When we understand, however, that the word "bad"
here is better understood as "evil," then we understand
that Jesus is not talking about an impaired organ affecting
visual sight. He is, instead, explaining what occurs when
our eyes are guided by an *impaired heart* that we depend
upon for sound *spiritual sight.* And it is that impaired heart

that makes bad eyes of such terrible consequence that Jesus would say, "How great is that darkness!"

Well think about it…how else could an eye be evil? An eye could no more be evil than a foot or an elbow—two appendages that have neither intrinsic goodness nor intrinsic badness unto themselves, but must be steered and controlled in order to affect either helpfulness or havoc.

Likewise, each one of us steers, controls, and *directs* our eyes. And *in what ways* we direct them, Jesus is teaching here, will affect whether we have shining light or deepest darkness within us.

Proverbs 17:24 says, "A discerning man keeps wisdom in view, but a fool's eyes wander to the ends of the earth." How led astray we can be at times by these portals to both the *outside world*—where the panorama of color, shape, dimension, and texture are observed—and portals to aid our own *inner world* of imagination, desire, passion, and determination.

In 2 Samuel 11:2, King David (initially unintentionally) observed Bathsheba bathing. She was beautiful, according to the story; and from that moment on, the results of his inquiry, confirming that Bathsheba was *married* (married, in fact, to one of David's own loyal foot soldiers), was irrelevant to David. *Nothing mattered* compared with satisfying the goal of what his eyes had taken mental snapshot of, and now were in lusty pursuit of.

The powerful pull of temptation for Eve at the inception of sin for all mankind, in Genesis 3:1–7, wooing her toward that which God had expressly forbidden, took hold when Eve "*saw*" (verse 6) that the fruit:

a) "was good for food"

b) "was pleasing to the eye"

c) "desirable for gaining wisdom"

It's interesting that the second aspect to the temptation (that it "was pleasing to the eye") is first ascribed to a *woman* when this has been tripping us *men* up far more often than the ladies, ever since. We males are the ones most often and repeatedly drawn to what is "pleasing to the eye."

Did you ever notice that Jesus never gives a bleak and unfavorable critical assessment without also presenting something within our control to *prevent or remedy* the sad, sorry consequence? That is no less the case in this instance, for our eyes *will submit* to our (Holy Spirit-aided) wisdom and willpower.

Like King David, Esau, and countless other men, we are nearly willing to hand over our very souls if not jarred out of sin's *eye-appealing* intoxication and grip. Let us, therefore, Men, *be wise with our eyes*—recognizing that when our eyes are bad, we are full of darkness, but when our eyes are good, we shall not stumble...for we are "full of light!"

The 23rd of the Month

*Therefore, confess your sins to each other and
pray for each other so that you may be
healed. The prayer of a righteous
man is powerful and effective.*

—JAMES 5:16

There are three kinds of confessions:

1) Confessions to God, as the One all sin first and
   foremost is offensive toward (see 2 Sam. 24:10,
   Neh. 1:6, Luke 15:18, Matt. 6:12, Psalm 38:18,
   Psalm 41:4, Psalm 51:4, Proverbs 28:13).

2) Confessions to the person we have directly sinned
   against (see Exod. 10:16, 1 Sam. 15:24–25, Matt.
   5:23–24, Luke 15:21, Luke 17:3).

3) And lastly, confessions to a third-party (an "inter-
   cessor" if you will), a trusted brother in Christ;
   perhaps a pastor or spiritual leader in the church
   (see 2 Sam. 12:13, Mark 1:5, Acts 8:24).

This third form is the confession Saint James is instructing
us here to have as a regular regime in our Christian faith
walk. James expects us in this instance to seek out a person

who is not the one you have sinned against, but rather a person who will receive you with compassion, humility, and wisdom in order that he would be willing and best prepared to pray for you.

This is the kind of nonjudgmental person the Apostle Paul refers to who would "restore [you] gently," humble in his own self-awareness that he too might be tempted in the *very same way* were he not ever watchful (Gal. 6:1). We're talking about a man you would not be too embarrassed to confess persistent lust, porn viewing, or any other sexual sin to.

This is a friend in which you may have established some *mutual* accountability with. Confessing to your pastor or spiritual leader is advisable and of great benefit in many cases, but I don't think this is the person that James is ideally speaking of here. That is because, in addition to our confession, his instructions include "and pray for each other."

Christians certainly should pray for their elders, pastor, or minister and these servant-leaders for us, but James seems to be indicating such relationship where the *confession* and prayer support is a *two-way* street—something that rarely occurs between clergy and their flock. Also, this is confession and prayer that involves serious failures, chronic sinful thoughts and behavior, which warrant James saying "so that you may be *healed.*"

For contrast's sake, we don't need to be "healed" of the sin of driving too fast when running late to an appointment. We don't need to be healed of daydreaming during Sunday morning sermons or of regularly dominating a meeting when the saints gather for Bible study and fellowship.

James advocates that this prayer-accountability partner is a person of personal righteousness. That only makes sense. We need an advocate who is well received at the Father's throne and is one who *believes* that he'll receive what he asks for on our behalf! That is why he says in the same breath, "the prayer of a *righteous man* is powerful and effective."

This is the kind of person who is willing to participate with you in the faithful and committed way that *mutually* you fulfill St. Paul's admonition: "Carry each other's burdens, and in this way you will fulfill the law of Christ" (Gal. 6:2).

This is a person who sees you regularly in order to know the pulse and pace of your Christian walk in the *best of times*, and so aptly understands the context of your weakness and temptation. And, therefore, he is at-the-ready (only a phone call or email away) to spring into action with prayer and support on a moment's notice in the *worst of times*.

I have been incalculably grateful that I have a few such good men in my life for accountability, and have had so for my entire Christian walk, which started at age 14. And I know they would view me in the same light regarding their lives—praise God!

The alternative to living a life of regular confession and accountability is keeping one's hidden sin life just that...*hidden*...and, consequently, living a lie, a life full of deception.

It is in those private dimly-lit places and choices that Satan reigns, and God's loving mercy and deliverance (the very thing the one with the sin stronghold needs most) is perpetually kept at arm's length.

This can be contrasted with walking into the light of transparency, honesty, and humility, remembering that "God opposes the proud but gives grace to the humble" (James 4:6); and that he "who conceals his sin does not prosper, but whoever confesses and renounces them finds mercy" (Prov. 28:13).

I pray that you would have the friend(s) who meet these qualifications and that you, in turn, would be such a brother to them—that you would have the *courage* to be transparent with them, unashamed and unafraid of condemnation, rejection, or compromised confidentiality. I pray that you would confess to them as often as needed and helpful in the area of sexual purity; and that, at such times, you would be *healed*.

The 24th of the Month

Those who live according to the sinful nature
have their minds set on what that nature desires;
but those who live in accordance with the Spirit
have their minds set on what the Spirit desires.

—ROMANS 8:5

The peerless Billy Graham was questioned at one point regarding the sin of lust and explained (I'm paraphrasing): "When you at first look and recognize that an attractive woman is in your presence, that's not a sin. It's taking that *second look* that is the sin."

This is precisely what the Apostle Paul in today's devotion is referring to—our giving in to lots of *second* looks. It is where your heart "sets" that God's concerned with, not our startled glances and wholesome recognition of someone's attractiveness.

Righteous Job of the oldest book in the Bible was given this extraordinary, virtually *unequaled*, commendation from God: "There is no one on earth like him; he is blameless and upright, a man who fears God and shuns evil" (Job 1:8). In chapter 31, verse 1 (KJV), Job says, "I made a covenant with mine eyes; why then should I think upon a maid?"

Evidence of Job's sterling character was his stalwart determination not to give in to lustful thoughts when in the presence of a woman. In eloquent and graceful language, Job considered his commitment to mental moral purity a *covenant with his eyes*—an internal promise to God *and himself* not to accept and entertain impure thoughts. In doing so, Job was taking the very same attitude that Billy Graham, many centuries later, was speaking about.

The Apostle Paul states in Galatians 5:17, "The sinful nature desires what is *contrary to the Spirit*, and the Spirit what is *contrary to the sinful nature*." Let's face it, Brothers, my flesh, your flesh, often desires things *contrary* to God's commandments, his desired will, and his ultimate best for us.

Our unspiritual manhood desires money, prestige, physical comforts, and sexual gratification. These are things that are not evil, in and of themselves, but when unrestrained and not guided by God's Spirit—his teachings and will for us—will mislead us to destructive ends. At such times, we will be motivated to strive for them without regard for whether they are obtained in a righteous manner, and regardless of whether they glorify God in our lives.

So how do you take a mind that is set on what the *sinful* nature desires and cooperate and assist in its transformation into a mind that is set on what the *Spirit* desires? To start off with, you must have the humility to conduct a non-defensive, honest, inner self-assessment regarding where your mind sets much of the time regarding godly and *ungodly* thinking. The wise Proverb 23:7 explains, "For as he *thinketh* in his heart, so is he" (KJV).

If quite regularly your mind is noticeably set on what the sinful nature desires, it's high time to disrupt that comfortable, familiar pattern of thinking. And that means it's long overdue to refamiliarize yourself with what *the Spirit desires*; to "fix these words of mine [of God's] in your hearts and *minds*" (Deut. 11:18), and to *hold on* to what Jesus has taught us. Jesus said, "If you *hold to my teaching*, you are really my disciples. *Then* you will know the truth, and the truth will set you free" (John 8:31–32).

Let's apply those words of Jesus in a beneficial and very practical way, as follows: it is impossible to "hold to" what Jesus has taught us while simultaneously having our minds *holding on* to what the sinful nature desires. Did you hear that?…

It is impossible *to hold to what Jesus has taught us while simultaneously having our minds holding on to what the sinful nature desires.* If your mind is set on impure thoughts and images, it's time to renew your grip and "hold" onto the teachings of Jesus Christ. And Christ promises here that his teaching (the "truth" he has offered to each one of us) will "set you free" (John 8:32).

Brothers, I ask you: do you genuinely desire to have your mind *set* on what the Spirit desires? I know that you do! Then "live in accordance with the Spirit" (Rom. 8:5); for when you "live by the Spirit…you will not gratify the desires of the sinful nature" (Gal. 5:16).

Ephesians 4:22–24 tells us to "*put off your old self*, which is being corrupted by its deceitful desires…and put on the new self, created to be like God in true righteousness and holiness." In that very passage, sandwiched between the admonitions of what needs putting off and putting on, is the work of the Spirit in that transaction, described as being "made new in the attitude of your minds."

None of us will succeed in putting off the old self and putting on the new, unless the Spirit renews our minds! That is something God's Spirit can, and will, do for us as we pray for this…yield to his Spirit in this…and "set" our minds on what his Spirit desires.

Finally, Brothers, *here* is where we ought to direct, center, and "set" our thoughts as much as possible: "Whatever is *true,* whatever is *noble,* whatever is *right,* whatever is *pure,* whatever is *lovely,* whatever is *admirable*—if anything is *excellent* or *praiseworthy*—*think about such things*" (Phil. 4:8).

Let us pray: Father God, we fall at your feet and humbly confess that we need a Holy Spirit extreme mind-makeover. We cannot in and of ourselves make new the attitude of our minds. If you don't do it, it won't happen. We determine this day, as never before, to cooperate with your Spirit to make new the attitude of our minds. We need his presence and power, strategy and strength, to have our minds set on what *your Spirit desires* instead of on what our old, stubbornly resilient, sinful nature desires. Help us this day and every day, Lord, to live according to your Spirit. In Christ's name, Amen.

The 25th of the Month

*Flee from sexual immorality. All other sins a man
commits are outside his body, but he who sins
sexually sins against his own body.*

—1 CORINTHIANS 6:18

Experts in the field of psychology determined many
years ago that when a human being is in a situation of
recognizable imminent danger, his body will have a "fight
or flight" response. In other words, *fight back* or *get away*!

The behavioral scientists believe a rational sizing up of
the threat and weighing one's reasonable chance for success
is not what happens initially, but instead an instantaneous
response of the autonomic nervous system of fight or flight.
A racing heartbeat, or involuntarily screaming and running,
would be examples of this that commonly occur when a
person is suddenly facing great peril.

According to God's Word, in the area of sexual sin
we are the threat to ourselves! With the great advantage
of spiritual insight, versus a behavioral sciences theorem,
the Apostle Paul advocates *flight* over fight, urging us to,
"Flee from sexual immorality." When it comes to sexual
temptation, our personal well-being is in mortal danger,
so in automatic, urgent, involuntary response, we are told
here to "escape!"

In reality, having the benefit of some time in most instances to assess the threat when tempted with impure thoughts and sexual sins, we can legitimately ask ourselves, "Since I am going to *harm myself* by these sexual thoughts or actions, why proceed any further?"

When Paul commended husbands to love their wives "as [they love] their own bodies" (Eph. 5:28–29), he explained that "After all, no one ever hated his own body, but he feeds and cares for it, just as Christ does the church."

There is a great irony, therefore, when we give in to sexual sins. We do so in an attempt to *care for own body*, yet the Word of God in 1 Corinthians 6:18 contradicts that, explaining, "he who sins sexually *sins against his own body*." We are in fact *not caring* for our own bodies at those times, but *harming ourselves*!

Similarly, Proverbs 6:32 teaches us that "a man who commits adultery lacks judgment; whoever does so *destroys himself*." Since Christ has warned us that to look lustfully upon a woman is to commit adultery in one's heart (Matt. 5:27–28), we are even in those cases of impure imaginations, little by little, chipping away at our inner man—degrading our souls, *destroying* ourselves.

Following Christ is sometimes like living in an alternate reality. It is a matter of choosing to follow the truth even when our physical senses or mental faculties tell us otherwise.

Proverbs 3:5 is perhaps the best Old Testament precursor to this principle when it says, "Trust in the Lord with all your heart and *lean not on your own understanding*." Another Old Testament example of this is found in Proverbs 14:12, which states, "There is a way which *seems right* to a man, but in the end it leads to death."

Jesus Christ constantly challenged his disciples in these paradoxical ways. Consider this smattering of samples: "The man who loves his life will lose it, while the man who hates his life in this world will keep it for eternal life" (John 12:25); "The spirit gives life; the flesh counts for nothing" (John 6:63); "Whoever finds his life will lose it, and whoever loses his life for my sake will find it" (Matt. 10:39); "But seek first his kingdom and his righteousness and all these things [regarding food and drink and clothing, bodily provisions] will be given to you as well" (Matt. 6:33).

I'm sure, at times, Jesus's disciples had a lot of furrowed brows and befuddled looks on their faces as Jesus was teaching them these things. They had so much that needed to be *unlearned,* as a matter of first course, in order to absorb these kingdom truths of vibrant Christ-follower living.

As contemporary disciples of Jesus Christ, we too must *unlearn* many of our natural inclinations—how we care for our own bodies in ways that seem most satisfying and urgently fulfilled. We need to believe once and for all that fulfilling our sexual impulses in *ANY* impure, unrighteous manner at all is *detrimental* to our well-being and, ironically, a form of hating ourselves!

Proverbs 3:7–8 states, "Do not be wise in your own eyes; fear the Lord and shun evil. *This will bring health to your body* and nourishment to your bones." That includes our *sexual* health and contentment. Bring about no harm to yourself this day, my Brothers!

The 26th of the Month

So if the Son sets you free, you will be free indeed.

—JOHN 8:36

Long before Abraham Lincoln's "Emancipation Proclamation," regarding the freeing of black slaves in America, Jesus gave us this *universal* emancipation proclamation:
"If the Son sets you free, you will be free indeed."

Only moments prior, Jesus diagnosed just exactly what
it is the human condition needs to be liberated from: "I tell
you the truth, everyone who sins is a slave to sin" (John 8:34).
Jesus's impetuous yet precious disciple, Peter, reiterated this
a few years later when he said, "a man is a *slave to whatever
has mastered him*" (2 Pet. 2:19).

Slaves are bound by physical chains of one kind or
another and/or they have psychological chains but, either
way, they are controlled and held captive. What Jesus is
saying is that if you sin repeatedly (*uncontrollably* as it were)
you are held *captive to sin*. You are in sin's grip, its power,
and yes, even its *service*. Jesus, on the other hand, offers us
our true, legal, and lasting freedom when he says, "If the
Son sets you free, you will be free indeed."

You see the master of an estate could set a slave free, but
if he had a firstborn son, that son might object and seek to
revoke the slave's release from bondage. As rightful legal

94

"heir" to the estate and all of its belongings, he might easily surmise that the slaves are *each one his* (eventually) and that the father is, in reality, compromising his inheritance by this clemency.

Therefore, if the *son* sets the slave free, there is no one left to repeal the slave's freedom. That is why Jesus says assuredly, "So if the *Son* sets you free, you will be free indeed!" We all need that kind of *irrevocable* freedom from sin's vise grip!

That is what Jesus Christ, and *only* Jesus Christ, offers us. He is the "only begotten Son," the inheritor of all that is the Father's (see Matt. 21:38). When Christ, therefore, has set us free—*because he is the Son*—we are free indeed!

Christ is not only interested in freeing us from sin's *penalty* (Hell) but also sin's *power* (bondage) over our lives. Since the Son has set us free, if we have become re-entangled in the sins of lust and impurity, it is our own doing!

Second Peter 2:22 reads, "Of them the proverbs are true: 'A dog returns to its vomit,' and, 'A sow that is washed goes back to her wallowing in the mud.'" In which case, the Apostle Peter says, he is worse off than if he never came to Christian faith in the first place: "If they have escaped the corruption of the world by knowing our Lord and Savior Jesus Christ and are *again entangled in it and overcome*, they are worse off at the end than they were at the beginning." (When able to fully review, see passages 2 Pet. 2:19–22, Psalm 85:8.)

Read Romans 6:22, 1 Corinthians 7:22, Ephesians 6:6, and Romans 6:18 and you will see that the only thing God wants us to be slaves to is Himself...to Christ, and to "righteousness." By the inner-working, *inner-living*, Spirit of the Lord there is freedom (see 2 Cor. 3:17).

So, Brothers, do not let yourselves be burdened again with a yoke of slavery to sexual sin in *any* of its forms. The Son has set you free; there is no one left to repeal his decision, and you are free indeed!

The 27th of the Month

*So I tell you this, and insist on it in the Lord,
that you no longer live as the Gentiles do, in the
futility of their thinking…Having lost all sensitivity, they have given themselves over to sensuality
so as to indulge in every kind of impurity,
with a continual lust for more.*

—EPHESIANS 4:17 AND 4:19

I t's only natural to perhaps mildly over-romanticize how
thrilling, how courageous and faithful, the times and
tenor of the first century church must have been. And
had we solely the absolute page-turner adventures of the
"Book of Acts" to capture the character and condition of
the church of that time, this lovely mental picture of ours
would be wholly undisturbed.

While the Acts stories will always tremendously inspire
us and evoke great imagination and admiration, passages
such as this one in Ephesians gives us another perspective.
And it's a sobering one—peering into a church made up
of very imperfect lives. It is a church comprised of at least
some number of believers with immature faith and compromised morals—that warrant the Apostle's ardent appeal
like this for purity.

How uncanny, how similar, people two thousand years

ago were to us in the church today, so *equally prone* to regressing to the ways of *unenlightened unbelievers*—in this context termed, "Gentiles."

What had happened in such a brief amount of time to their faith? To their power and *resolve* that Paul must implore them (*"insist"* upon) that they "no longer live as the Gentiles do?"

What has happened to *our* faith when we equally compromise, Brothers? What has diminished our resolve, and the memories of our lives *before* Christ, that the Holy Spirit must keep conducting the Lord's course correction in our lives?

Hadn't the Ephesian believers made up their minds *long* before this, once and for all, who they were to going follow: the Risen Savior, Lord of the Universe, and Lover of their Souls? *Haven't we entirely made up our minds to follow our Lord and Savior in unwavering devotion?*

The last thing any of us needs again is to be lost in the "futility of [our] thinking." The problem is when we become *desensitized*, as they did, "having lost all sensitivity" (Eph. 4:19), we do not comprehend how futile our thinking has become.

Jesus was dismayed in Matthew 11:17 over the robotic desensitized people surrounding him: "We played the flute for you, and you did not dance; we sang a dirge and you did not mourn." Once desensitized to the subtle yet undeniable prickling and procession of God's Word and Spirit in our lives, we're vulnerable to "indulge in every kind of impurity, with a continual lust for more."

Anyone of us that has ever given in to sexual temptation knows how ultimately unsatisfying it is. And God's Word, by saying such indulgence leads to "a continual lust for more," is sounding an alarm here, Brothers! God's Word is making it crystal clear that giving in to such temptations shall *never satiate* the true need; in fact, it will actually *increase* the desires and drumbeat of the demands of the flesh. It is not unlike the person marooned at sea who invariably drinks sea water, only to find that it makes him even more thirsty!

Many years ago, late into the night and watching TV past any semblance of good judgment by doing so, a very impure commercial came on. They were selling a DVD monthly subscription to some kind of real-life, nonactor, scenes of immorality and nudity.

What I have never forgotten was how the first month's DVD was offered at *no charge* at all! The makers of this video indecency had discovered what God had told in his timeless Word many generations ago—that to indulge in such impurity ensures "the continual lust for more." And, therefore, the deceived subscribers would readily pay for the subsequent months—out of *compulsion* even more than perverse curiosity.

You know, my friends, there is clearly a longing within each one of us needing to be satisfied. It's a universal condition, and it's not sexual.

Our longing and thirst, at its core, *is for Jesus.* Psalm 27:8 explains, "My heart says of you, 'Seek his face!' Your face, LORD, I will seek." And I believe that Saint Augustine (living in the fourth and fifth centuries) spoke for all of us when he diagnosed the universal condition this way: "our heart is restless until it finds its rest in thee."

Jesus answered the plea of St. Augustine's heart—and truly each one of ours—when he said, "Come to me, all you who are weary and burdened, and I will give you rest...

rest for your souls" (Matt. 11:28–29). Jesus alone was able, and thrilled, to say, "If anyone is thirsty, *let him come to me and drink*" (John 7:37). Jesus alone is able to satisfy the deepest longing in our souls that we would, *fully satisfied*, "no longer live as the Gentiles [ones apart from God] do."

The 28th of the Month

*Therefore, there is now no condemnation for
those who are in Christ Jesus.*

—ROMANS 8:1

Struggling with issues of pornography, or even persistent lust, for the Christian man is thoroughly demoralizing. There are few sins that can throw one's confident good standing with God into such mental uncertainty and troubled conscience. Nagging, troubling doubts about whether God still loves and accepts you are part and parcel of the struggle. In remarkable similarity, King David bellowed in pained anguish, "My iniquities have overtaken me so that *I am not able to look up.* They are more than the hairs on my head; therefore *my heart fails me*" (Psalm 40:12 , World English Bible).

There are thirty other devotions in this series—each one dedicated to spur one another on in righteousness till conformed to the image of God's Son (see Rom. 8:29). This one, however, is strictly dedicated to reinforcing and reminding us of God's unconditional love and forgiveness— his unrelenting acceptance of us as his children.

How we should rest in such serene knowledge, trust, and contentment when we consider the deep and abiding, *lavish* love our Heavenly Father has for each one of us!

Deeply drink this in, Brothers: "How great is the love the Father has lavished on us, that we should be called children of God!" (1 John 3:1). Psalm 103:11–12 reads, "For as high as the heavens are above the earth, *so great is his love* for those who fear him; as far as the east is from the west, so far has he *removed our transgressions from us.*"

Jesus said in Mark 3:28–29, "I tell you the truth, all the sins and blasphemes of men will be forgiven them. But whoever blasphemes against the Holy Spirit will never be forgiven; he is guilty of an eternal sin." What precisely it means to "blaspheme the Holy Spirit" has been dissected and debated by gaggles of theological minds (far superior to mine) down through the ages. That is not what we're interested in getting at here.

What I want you to zero in on, Brothers, is this stupendous (all at once scintillating while serene) truth, when Jesus said:

ALL SINS AND BLASPHEMES OF MEN WILL BE FORGIVEN THEM!

Perhaps your unsubdued sexual impulses have already led to the breakup of a marriage or two in your life. As unfortunate and regrettable as that is, it certainly can be forgiven. Divorce is not the unforgivable sin. It is not blasphemy of the Holy Spirit. *Every single one of your sins involving sexuality is forgivable.*

That is, after all, why Jesus died for us—to take away the sins of the world (see John 1:29); "For God did not send his Son into the world to condemn the world but to save the world through him" (John 3:17). The Apostle Paul put it concisely: "I do not set aside the grace of God, for if righteousness could be gained through the law, Christ died for nothing!" (Gal. 2:21).

And Romans 5:7–9 explains: "Very rarely will anyone die for a righteous man, though for a good man someone might possibly dare to die. But God demonstrates his own love for us in this: While we were still sinners, Christ died for us. Since we have now been justified by his blood, how much more shall we be saved from God's wrath through him!"

Love "keeps no record of wrongs" (1 Cor. 13:5). That includes our keeping active reminders *unto ourselves* of our own sins. To continue to do so is to not love *one's self,* which is in direct opposition to what Jesus wanted for us when he taught, "Love your neighbor *as yourself*" (Mark 12:31).

What we, instead, need to constantly remind ourselves of is this: "Whoever comes to me I will never drive away" (John 6:37). And we'd do well to gratefully bring to mind 1ˢᵗ John 2:1 at times of particular shame: "My dear children, I write this to you so that you will not sin. But if anybody does sin, we have one who speaks to the Father in our defense—Jesus Christ, the Righteous One."

"Because of the LORD's great love we are not consumed, for his compassions never fail. They are *new every morning*; great is your faithfulness" (Lam. 3:22–23). And "if we confess our sins, he is faithful and just and *will forgive us our sins* and purify us from all unrighteousness" (1 John 1:9). Did you catch that? He not only forgives us, but as we come to him in confession, he continually *purifies* us. He *forgives and cleanses* us.

"Therefore, if anyone is in Christ, he is *a new creation*; the old has gone, the new has come!" (2 Cor. 5:17). Do you feel like a new creation this day, Brother? It's true…you are one! The old is dead and gone. Rejoice!

Let us pray: Once again, thank you so much, Father God, for Jesus's dying on our behalf. Thank you that your compassions are new *every* morning. The old is dead and gone; behold, we are anew! Thank you for loving us while we were yet sinners and now, as your beloved children, loving us all the more! Thank you for never giving up on us, no matter how many times we fail you. You will never drive us away. Thank you for not only forgiving us but continually purifying us. We happily receive your love. We love you back, Abba God! In Christ's name, Amen.

The 29th of the Month

The thief comes only to steal and kill and destroy;
I have come that they may have life,
and have it to the full.

—JOHN 10:10

Satan is such a thief. How many things, days, and doings of God's best for you has he already stolen from you? No more!

Satan is such a killer—in truth, and according to Jesus, a "murderer from the beginning" (John 8:44); and, to this day, Satan is intent to murder your faith! How many times have you doubted and faltered in your faith at his evil instigation? No more!

Satan is such a destroyer: a destroyer of dreams and such a consummate liar. Actually, "there is no truth in him. When he lies, he speaks his native language, for he is a liar and the father of lies" (John 8:44). He is lying to you, *regularly*, in the areas of sexuality. How often have you cozied up a little closer to hear the lies about what might really satisfy you sexually? No more!

With Satan and his minion evil spirits' enterprise of spiritual and moral theft, murder, and destruction (intent to "steal, kill, and destroy") lurking at every corner, Jesus offers us the only antiserum—Zoë (pronounced *zoh aye*).

That is the "life" only found in God! Jesus triumphantly announced, "I have come that they may have zoë, and have it to the full!"

Now largely extinct, the language of ancient Greece (so much richer than ours) had three words that we English-speaking persons merely translate as *life*. "Bios," the first of these, represents the *biological* life in all living matter, present in human and animal and plant life.

Next, "psuche" (pronounced *sue kay*) is the *psychological* life that exists in the soul of a person, yet not within the pine cone.

And last of all, there is "zoë," which is the *spiritual* life only found in God. So wonderfully, it is imparted to believers as a gift from God, and evidence of the *living presence of God* within us! It is the irrefutable, irrevocable life in the "spirit" that Jesus offers each and every repentant, open heart to him (see John 3:5–6).

Zoë is what the Apostle Paul excitedly referred to as *"the life that is truly life"* (1 Tim. 6:19). *This*, my friends, is the "life" Jesus speaks of when he says, "I have come that they may have *zoë*, and have it to the full!"

Jesus knew he didn't need to come to bring us *bios*. We already had that.

Jesus knew he didn't need to come to bring us *psuche*. We *already had that*.

But Jesus loved us so very much, and knew that *he had to come* in order that we would have *zoë*! Hallelujah, and thank you, Lord!

When we are tempted, Brothers, we need to pull out our zoë dipstick to see how "full" the zoë life of God is within us; for Jesus ardently says here that he wants us to "have it *to the full*." When our zoë is not to the full line, we are wide open to give in to temptation we, otherwise, would have no interest in. We are vulnerable because we are not full up, in and with, the zoë life in the Spirit!

Jesus told the (zoë-less) Samaritan woman at the well, "Everyone who drinks this water will be thirsty again, but whoever drinks the water I give him will never thirst. Indeed, the water I give him will become in him a spring of water welling up to eternal life" (John 4:13–14). She was clueless to the fact that Jesus was talking about a *spiritual* refreshment; something no well on earth could supply.

That is why she responded quite naturally, "Sir, give me this drink so that I won't get thirsty and have to keep coming here to draw water" (John 4:15). She wanted no further labor, and public embarrassment, from coming for her liquids in the heat of the day.

Brothers, we have received the new drink from the Lord's own ladle! We have within each one of us the "spring of water welling up to eternal life," *LIVING WATER,* as it were (see John 4:10; John 7:38).

So why don't we act like it? Why would we ever continue to live and act as if we were as parched and empty as this woman here presently on her sixth lover? When we look upon a woman impurely, aren't we on our 1,006th lover?

"As the deer pants for streams of water, so my soul pants for you, O God. My soul thirsts for God, for the living God. When can I go and meet with God?" (Psalm 42:1–2). These words were penned by a man like you and me—a man who *yearns* for God—with one exception: the Psalmist did not have the "living water," the quenching Holy Spirit, interacting with his own spirit as we do. *Our thirst should never approximate his!*

Do you need zoë to the full (*"abundantly"* KJV) this day? For any one of us, if this is so, here is what must be asked of oneself, as the Psalmist asked, "When can I go and meet with God?"

How soon can I get alone with Him in my prayer closet? How soon can I spend priority uninterrupted time reading, meditating upon, his Holy Word? How soon can I go and worship him in the presence and fellowship of his Son's living body, the church?

"Whom have I in heaven but you? And earth has nothing I desire besides you" (Psalm 73:25). The Disciple Peter echoed this so perfectly when he said, "Lord, to whom shall we go? You have the words of eternal life. We believe and know that you are the Holy One of God" (John 6:68–69).

Let us pray: Father God, help us find and always remember our sole sufficiency is in you. You not only bring us the words of life, you give us life—*zoë*, spiritual life itself. And as *living water* within us, we need not ever thirst again! Help us not only to believe this in our minds but receive and recognize this daily in our souls—that we would never seek to be filled with other, *impure*, things, which can never quench our spirit's thirst as You alone can. In Christ's name, Amen.

The 30th of the Month

Why embrace the bosom of another man's wife?
For a man's ways are in full view of the Lord,
and he examines all his paths.

—PROVERBS 5:20–21

These provocative words were originally presented by King Solomon when there were no televisions, there were no movies, there was no Internet…and women dressed in nearly universal nonattention-grabbing modesty. Solomon, nonetheless, keenly understood how the male's rapt attention to the female's curvaceous anatomy would represent the precursor to a great many sins.

Nowadays, scantily clad well-shaped women are unashamedly emphasized in, what certainly feels like, 50% of the commercials on television—selling beer, selling cars, perfumes, the latest motion picture advertisement, woman's underclothes (of course) etc.—not to mention the *actual* TV shows and movies we have to select from. It's a national obsession of sorts. My wife has said on more than one occasion, "Hollywood has no mercy on wives!"

As we've already fully established, Jesus views lusting in one's heart for a woman some equivalence to committing unauthorized sex with her (see Matt. 5:27–28). Consequently, Solomon poses a very current question to us: why embrace, even figuratively speaking (visually and mentally, versus *literally*), the bosom of another man's wife? Why do it?... and especially when God knows our thoughts (see Psalms 94:11).

Sometimes the little conjunction words (*and, but, for*) in the Bible are actually the product-key to discovering the message God is trying to get across. Today's passage is one of those instances. Right after the provocative, piercing question we are considering, Solomon uses the conjunction *for*, and it enables us to comprehend exactly what we need to walk away with here:

"Why embrace the bosom of another man's wife, *for*" [when/whereby/in light of the fact] "a man's ways are in full view of the Lord, and he examines all his paths."

Brothers, I am sure we would contentedly go along continually to lust—*slyly* when a live attractive woman is physically near to us, and *brazenly* when a woman is undressed or undressing on our motion picture, television, or computer screens—if no one knew about it except ourselves, and we had *no fear* of any detrimental consequence. That is not the case, thank God.

We think we're the only ones doing the watching? Not so! The Lord is watching also. Our ways are in "full view of the Lord." We are delighting in something we are viewing, and the Lord is *not delighting in the least* in what he is viewing—us in our sin!

He says, "I supplied all their needs, yet they committed adultery and thronged to the houses of prostitutes. They are well-fed, lusty stallions, *each neighing for another man's wife*" (Jer. 5:7–8). There it is again: lusting after "*another man's wife.*" This is the *exact same wording* as in our devotion today!

When we make imprudent choices in entertainment including nudity and sex scenes—and do not simply look away, choose to turn it off completely, hit the "skip" button, or walk out of the room for a bit—we too have "thronged to the houses of prostitutes" of Jeremiah 5:7. And the reality is, we have been duped into accepting that a movie that is 100% graphic sex scenes is "X-rated" or "porn," but the R-rated movie with only a 2-minute (soft porn) sex scene is acceptable "entertainment," and represents something essential to the story.

Unless he lives completely alone, a man with a daily Internet porn addiction—or even a *sporadic* dalliance problem with it—will nearly always cover his tracks. He'll erase his web history and delete the cookies. He'll attempt to remove and destroy "all of his paths" that he has traveled on.

Yet remember, Brothers, we have a loving all-knowing, *all-seeing*, God; and our passage here assures us, "he examines *all* his paths" (Prov. 5:21). A delete button hasn't been invented (and never will be) that can successfully obscure, remove, or destroy what God chooses to examine.

That is why Solomon asks the "rhetorical" question, "Why embrace the bosom of another man's wife?" It is *rhetorical* in that he's not really asking a question to elicit any defense; he's saying, "Don't do it, Brothers!" *For a man's ways are in full view of the Lord.*

111

The 31ˢᵗ of the Month

Above all else, guard your heart,
for it is the wellspring of life.

—PROVERBS 4:23

The phrase "above all" appears sixteen times in the NIV Bible, but the phrase "above all else" does not appear anywhere else except solely here in Proverbs 4:23. I think it's safe to say then that what follows is more than a little bit important.

No one would have been in the least surprised if God's Word had said, above all else, *love one another!* Or above all else, *pray without ceasing!* Or surely, above all else, *have faith in God!* Instead God said, "Above all else, guard your heart, for it is the wellspring of life."

The heart is the "wellspring of life" because the heart is the seat and center and sustenance of who *we've been,* who *we are,* and who we *are to become.* Most important, it is where Christ Jesus, himself, astoundingly takes up residence. In the *believing* heart (see Eph. 3:17), and where God's love dwells in us by faith: "God has poured out his love *into our hearts* by the Holy Spirit" (Rom. 5:5).

For years I wondered why in Luke 5:22 Jesus (reading their minds) asks the Pharisees, "Why are you thinking these things *in your hearts?*" Everyone knows our minds, our brains, conduct thought. Right?

So why didn't Jesus ask, "Why are you thinking these things *in your minds?*" Elsewhere, in Matthew 15:19, Jesus does it again, teaching his disciples that "out of the *heart* come evil thoughts" (versus thoughts emanating out of the *mind*). And evidently his disciple Peter learned this very well, for later on Peter rebuked "Simon the Sorcerer" for "such a [wicked] thought *in your heart*" (Acts 8:22).

Our minds are like computer storage devices and computer processors in the sense that they actuate thinking (*computing*, so to speak); but the source and sustenance of our thinking is not in an organ at all. Instead, it resides in that mysterious inner seat-of-one's-soul, nether place the Bible refers to as our "hearts."

Consequently, we need to protect the spiritual integrity of our hearts more than a SWAT team protects their physical heart organs with body armor. We need to be wise *in our hearts* at avoiding temptations: "The prudent man sees danger and takes refuge, but the simple keep going and suffer for it" (Prov. 22:3).

Brothers, I implore you *not to keep going* in any areas you've been compromising in regarding sexual purity. *You don't want you to suffer for it:* "In the paths of the wicked lie thorns and snares, but he who *guards his soul* stays far from them" (Prov. 22:5).

The Holy Spirit is there for us in order to *help us* guard our hearts. Let's not disqualify ourselves then from his help by holding on to "eye candy," *clinging* on to worldliness: "Those who cling to worthless idols *forfeit the grace* that could be theirs" (Jonah 2:8). Actually, the very same verse in the King James Bible presents, in my opinion, this even more potent warning concerning porn: "They that *observe lying vanities* forsake their own mercy."

Instead, Brothers, let us "throw off *everything that hinders* and the sin that so easily entangles, and let us run with perseverance the race marked out for us" fixing "our eyes *on Jesus*" (Heb. 12:1–2).

Pornographic temptation is a danger, a snare, and *a worthless idol* all balled up in one. Were I to fall prey to this danger and snare—this spiritual *Kryptonite*—my spiritual life would be robbed of its highest fulfillment and my life, in its entirety, deprived of God's highest purposes for me. I believe King Lemuel, warning us in Proverbs 31:3, had something like that in mind when he said, "do not spend your strength on women, your vigor on those *who ruin kings.*"

My greatest fear is that at the end of my life, when my "flesh and body are spent," I would in pained agony of soul mourn, "How I hated discipline! How *my heart* spurned correction. I would not obey my teachers or listen to my instructors. I have come to the brink of utter ruin in the midst of the whole assembly" (Prov. 5:11–14).

I cannot—*will not*—let that happen. No, "*The Lord will fulfill his purpose for me*" (Psalm 138:8). I intend (with God's sure and able help) to *guard my heart*, to die at complete peace, in anticipation of the joy in hearing, "Well done, good and faithful servant!" Won't you join me?

If you would like to contact Peter:
RPWAuthor@TruthfulBooks.com

Printed in Great Britain
by Amazon

76111732R00071

C000017447

NICOLS

Best Walks
on the
ISLE OF SKYE

by Richard Hallewell

NICOLSON MAPS
3 Frazer St, Largs
Tel. 01475 689242

First published 1998 by Collins
An imprint of HarperCollins*Publishers*
77-85 Fulham Palace Road
London W6 8JB

© HarperCollinsPublishers 1998
Maps © Bartholomew Ltd 1998

The walks in this guide were first published in
Bartholomew's *Walk Skye and Wester Ross.*

All rights reserved. No part of this publication may be reproduced,
stored in a retrieval system, or transmitted in any form or by any
means, electronic, mechanical, photocopying, recording, or
otherwise, without the prior written consent of the Publisher and
copyright owner.

The landscape is changing all the time. While every care has been
taken in the preparation of this guide, the Publisher accepts no
responsibility whatsoever for any loss, damage, injury or
inconvenience sustained or caused as a result of using this guide.

ISBN 1 86097 054 0

MG10364

CONTENTS

Symbols

WC   Public conveniences available at route, or in nearby town. (NB: these facilities are often closed in winter.)

👢   Hill walking equipment required. Strong boots; warm waterproof clothing; map and compass for hill routes.

🐕   Route suitable for dogs.

🚌   Public transport available to this route. Details given on individual routes.

Grade

A   Requires a high level of fitness and – for the hill routes – previous experience of hill walking. The use of a detailed map is advised.

B   Requires a reasonable level of fitness. Book map sufficient.

C   A simple, short walk on good paths.

Key map for the walks

Key to map symbols

••••	Route	••▸•	Direction of route	**1 foot = 0.3m**
———	Metalled Road	wc	Public convenience	**1 mile = 1.6km**
++++++	Railway	▲▲	Coniferous woodland	
Ⓟ	Parking	♦♦	Broad-leaved woodland	
(50m)	Contour: shaded area is above height indicated	i	Tourist information centre	

4

INTRODUCTION

ABOUT THIS BOOK

This is a book of walks, each of which can be completed within one day. Each route is graded according to its level of difficulty, and wherever specialist hill walking equipment is required this is specified. There is a description of each route, including information on the character and condition of the paths, and with a brief description of the major points of interest along the way. In addition there is a sketch map of the route. Car parks, where available, are indicated on the route maps. The availability of public conveniences and public transport on particular routes is listed on the contents page, and at the head of each route. The suitability or otherwise of the route for dogs is also indicated on the contents page. The location of each route within the area is shown on the key map, and a brief description of how to reach the walk from the nearest town is provided at the start of each walk. National grid references are provided on the maps. The use of a detailed map, in addition to this book, is advised on all grade A walks.

Before setting out, all walkers are asked to read through the section of Advice to Walkers at the end of the Introduction. In the long term it never pays to become lax in taking safety precautions.

THE AREA

(Numbers in italics refer to individual walks.)
Like most of northern Scotland, the area is on the very edge of the area of comfortable human habitation: the population is small, and settlements are scattered thinly on the low land by the coast and along the occasional fertile glen.

When the last Ice Age retreated, some 8000 years ago, a landscape was revealed of steep-sided hills separated by wide valleys. The hills had been scraped down to the rock by the action of the glaciers: cracked and torn into dramatic peaks and narrow, broken ridges. The valleys were gouged into broad, U-shaped profiles, and were filled, in places, by saltwater inlets and freshwater lochs. The land was a poor, infertile one, but the landscape was, and remains, heroic in scale and form.

The Isle of Skye (apart from the Torridonian sandstone and gneiss of the southern part of the island) is composed of igneous rocks: basalt, granite and gabbro, formed when the molten magma from the interior of the Earth emerged onto the surface and cooled. These are hard rocks, which have produced, in places, some very dramatic effects: notably in the ridge of Trotternish (*5,6*) and the Cuillin Hills.

The island measures some 50 miles (80km) from Rubha Hunish in the north to the Point of Sleat (*9*) in the south, and around 25 miles (40km) at its widest point, between Neist Point (*1*) in the west and the eastern coast of Trotternish. The coastline is greatly indented, however, and the total land area is only around 670 square miles. The island is generally mountainous, but the peaks are low outside the tight group which constitutes the Cuillins: a tangled mass of rocky summits, ridges and corries, whose skyline is one of the finest sights in the Highlands. None of the routes in this guide enters the range (some experience of climbing is needed before venturing onto the steep slopes), but two of them (*10,11*) pass close by and provide fine views.

The main sea lochs around the island are Loch Snizort and Loch Dunvegan (*2*) in the north, and Lochs Bracadale (*13*), Scavaig (*10*) and Slapin in the west. The only large freshwater loch is Loch Coruisk, in the Cuillins, but there are numerous small rivers which are famous for their salmon and trout.

What little arable land there is is largely confined to the small-scale crofts along the coastal strip. The rest of the island is given over to rough sheep and cattle grazing, moorland and some forestry. The small population is scattered thinly around the coast of the island, sometimes collected into small crofting townships, but only forming towns at the island capital of Portree (*7*), and (to a lesser degree) at Dunvegan (*2*), Broadford and Kyleakin.

There are many smaller islands off the coast of Skye. The largest of these is Raasay (*8*), in the Inner Sound, which can only be reached by ferry from Skye. Amongst the many smaller, uninhabited islands is Oronsay (*13*) in Loch Bracadale, which can be reached on foot at low tide.

HISTORY

The earliest known inhabitants of the area were the Picts, whose various tribes occupied all of northern Scotland. They posed a serious threat to the northern boundaries of Roman occupation in Britain, yet their culture and language were subsequently to disappear almost entirely. They may have been of Celtic origin, but it is impossible to know for certain, and the only relics which they left were some items of metalwork, a collection of impressive stone carvings of uncertain purpose, and the advanced defensive structures known as brochs.

The carvings are thought to have been produced between the 6th and the 10th centuries. The earlier examples are decorated with abstract symbols and schematic animal forms, and may have represented family or tribal relationships; the later stones carry religious motifs.

The broch was a circular dry-stone tower, probably varying from 15 to 50 feet (4.6-15.2m) in height and with a single entrance. It was a defensive structure of the crudest form (presumably used as a refuge for surrounding tribesmen), yet the skill shown in the construction is often considerable.

The best examples in this area are Dun Telve and Dun Troddan, within a short distance of each other east of Glenelg (on the mainland), which are now retained in a well-preserved condition. Two less complete examples can be found near the path to Waternish Point on Skye (3).

From the 6th century onwards the Pictish communities throughout Scotland were increasingly on the defensive; harried in the south by the Britons and the Angles, and in the west by the Scots: a Celtic warrior-aristocracy which arrived from Ireland around 500 and established itself in the small kingdom of Dalriada in Argyll. The Scots were Gaelic-speaking and Christian, and their language and culture would gradually colonise virtually all of the area of modern Scotland.

In part, this was made possible by a further threat to all the tribes of Scotland: the increasing raids on the north and west, from around 800 onwards, by the Vikings. These coastal attacks affected both the Scots and the Picts, who seem to have moved inland under the pressure and may have been forced to work in concert to defend their territories. In 843 this trend was taken to its logical conclusion and the two kingdoms were unified under the Scot, Kenneth McAlpin.

The Vikings, meanwhile, established themselves in the northern and western islands, and (to a lesser extent) on the adjacent mainland. In succeeding generations they mingled with the existing populations of Picts and Scots to produce the mixed race of the Gallgaels. The resulting cultural mix varied from area to area: in the Northern and Western Isles the population largely adopted Norse language and customs, but elsewhere the earlier cultures survived in parallel (this seems to have occurred in Skye).

Nevertheless, the Hebrides remained under the overlordship of the Norwegian crown until after Alexander III had defeated King Haakon of Norway at the Battle of Largs (1263). Following this, Gaelic language and culture gradually ousted the Norse influence, until it had completely disappeared from Highlands and western islands.

The net result of these various invasions was to create a society with strong warlike traditions and a disinclination to accept the nominal central control of the Scottish monarchy; a control which the monarchy – Norman and increasingly anglicised – could never fully enforce. As a result, a distinctive social organisation developed north of the Highland Line – tribal and semi-anarchic – which would survive until the greater powers of the Crown and Parliament of Great Britain could be turned against it in the 18th century.

The clan system emerged around the 13th century. It was based upon the unit of the family group – clann means children – and although it became flexible to the extent that individuals, or indeed whole clans, could ally themselves to a local power irrespective of any family relationship, the notion of kinship remained a part of the idea of the clan, and made the relationship between the chief and his clansmen different from the more strictly legal ties binding (for example) a feudal overlord and his vassal.

Warfare was part of the culture of the Highlanders, and although it would be inaccurate to suggest that the clansmen were perpetually at war with each other, it is true that feuding was endemic, and that individual inter-clan wars could be of very long duration. No single power ever evolved in the

Highlands which was sufficiently strong to enforce a lasting peace, so disputes could only be ended by either the complete victory of one of the antagonists or the intervention of neighbouring clans.

The nearest thing to a central government of Gaelic Scotland was the Lordship of the Isles: a hereditary title held by the MacDonalds. It was based upon the memory of Norse independence in the islands, but at its height extended to include much of the Gaelic-speaking mainland. A plot entered into by John of the Isles (whereby the Lordship would become an independent kingdom beneath the overlordship of the English king) led ultimately to the forfeiture of the title to the Scottish Crown in 1493. Thereafter, the Highlands lacked any single power strong enough to ensure internal stability.

There were a number of branches of the powerful Clan Donald within this area: the MacDonalds of Sleat (9), in the south of Skye (the Clan Donald museum is at Armadale), and also in the north of the island in Trotternish (5,6), from where they expelled the MacLeods; the MacDonells of Glengarry, with their main stronghold at Invergarry on Loch Oich; and the MacDonalds of Clanranald in the southwest. In addition to these, the main clans in the region were the MacLeods in the west of Skye, where Dunvegan remains the seat of the chief, (2) and in Raasay (8), and the Mackinnons in the east of the island.

Following the defeat of the Jacobites at Culloden, in 1746, clan society and the culture which it fostered began to disintegrate. The chiefs became landlords rather than the fathers of their tribe, and discovered a more pressing need for funds than for armed clansmen – particularly as these could no longer bear arms. Those who wished to continue the tradition of following a fighting life joined the newly formed Highland regiments and fought abroad for the Hanoverian monarchy; those who didn't left for the factories in the south or emigrated to the New World, either willingly or otherwise. In the Highlands, the inland glens were largely cleared for sheep farming, and the population was moved down to the coast.

PLACE NAMES

Most of the place names in the area covered by this guide are Gaelic: a language now known to comparatively few (though you will probably hear it spoken on Skye). A knowledge of the more common elements can add to the pleasure of walking in the area, and can also be of some help in map reading – a short list is included below. Even now, a certain amount of guesswork will be required, as the words which appear on the map will, as often as not, be slightly different from those shown here. In the more isolated areas of the west, where the language is still spoken, the names will be more grammatically correct, and will thus be altered by aspiration, the addition of letters to denote case, etc.

Gaelic is not the only language to have been spoken in this area, and place names can suggest the extent of the influence of the various peoples who have inhabited this part of Scotland through the centuries. Having said that, there are limitations to the effectiveness of this system: the Picts – who once inhabited all of this area; though not, presumably, in large numbers – have left virtually no indication of their presence in this form.

The Vikings were rather more influential, and a number of quite common Norse elements can be found; particularly in Skye and on the western seaboard. *Dale* for valley, *-ay* for an island (Raasay, Oronsay), *-val* for a hill (Stockval, Healabhal: both in Skye), *-nish* for a headland (Trotternish, Ullnish, etc). These can sometimes be found with added Gaelic elements (Healabhal Mhor), while occasionally the Norse word has simply been adopted by the Gaelic language (Sgeir from the Norse *Sker*).

Common elements in place names (Gaelic unless otherwise stated):
aber – confluence
abhainn – river
acarsaid – harbour
ach/Achadh – field
allt – burn
aird – promontory
-ay/-ey – island (Norse)
bal/baile – town, settlement
beag/beg – small
bealach – hill pass
beinn/ben – mountain
breac – speckled
buidhe – yellow
camas – bay
carn/cairn – hill, heap of stones
cnoc/knock – hillock

coire – corrie (hollow)
creag/craig – rock, cliff
dale/dal – valley (Norse)
dubh – black
dun – steep hill, fort
eilean – island
firth – arm of the sea (Norse)
glas – Grey
inver – river mouth
kil – church
kyle/caol – narrow strait
leacann – slope
leitir – extensive slope
lochan – small loch
meall – rounded hill
mor – big
ruadh – red
rubha – point of land
sgeir/skerry – rock surrounded by sea
sgurr – peak, sharp top
sron – nose, point
stac – rocky column, cliff
storr – steep, high peak
tobar – well
-val – mountain (Norse)

NATURAL HISTORY

In order to describe the wildlife of the region, it is useful to provide a number of broad headings for the various habitats – **mountains and moorland**, **seashore**, **conifer woodland**, **broadleaved woodland** – and then to note the particular birds and animals which the walker may expect to see in each.

Mountains and moorland (3,4,5,6,8,9,10,11, 12,14). With the poor soils and heavy rainfall in the western part of the Highlands, moorland – generally confined to the higher slopes in the east – often remains the prevalent land cover right down to sealevel. Some **ptarmigan**, the hardiest of the grouse family, may be seen on the higher slopes, or lower in winter, but little else.

On the lower moors **red grouse** are present, with some **black grouse** (generally on the margins of woodland). The **wheatear** is common throughout the area during the summer, while the **stonechat** is present throughout the year. Of the waders, **snipe**, **curlew**, **golden plover**, **redshank** and **greenshank** are present, as are three types of falcon – **peregrine**, **kestrel** and **merlin** – plus the **buzzard**, **hen harrier**, **short-eared owl** and **golden eagle**. This latter is not uncommon amongst the higher hills. **Crows** are also present: some **carrion crows**, but more generally the **hooded crow** and the **raven**.

The largest wild mammal in Britain is the **red deer**. These stay high in the hills during the summer – partly to escape the fierce insect life of the summer moors – but return to the lower moors during the winter. There are also local colonies of **sika deer** and **wild goats**. These last are not truly wild, but are the descendants of domestic animals, although individual herds may be of some antiquity. Carnivores include **wildcat**, **fox** and **stoat**, while the **mountain hare** – which, like the **ptarmigan** and **stoat** turns white in the winter – can also be found on the moors.

Seashore (1,2,7,9,10,11,12,13,14). The foreshore is generally of rocks (1,7,9,13) or cliffs (1,11,12,13) and one fine coral beach (2).

Rock type and boulder size have some effect on the life of the rocky foreshores, but the most important element is the degree of exposure to heavy seas. On exposed beaches the cover is limited to **lichens** and **barnacles**, while, in the sheltered lochs, there is a greater density of **seaweeds**, plus **mussels**, **limpets** and other shellfish. **Crabs** are common between the high and low water marks, while **sea urchins** and **starfish** can be seen just below the lowest tides. The shells of **scallops** and other bivalves are often thrown up along the beaches.

The **common seal** is the sea mammal most likely to be seen; lying on rocky islands and points. In addition, **otters** can sometimes be seen swimming in the sea; particularly in the evening.

Bird life includes a variety of gulls (**herring**, **common**, **black-headed**, **greater blackback** and **kittiwake**) and **terns** (common and arctic), plus **fulmar** and **gannet** around the cliffs, along with **razorbill**, **guillemot**, **puffin**, **cormorant** and **shag**. Waders include **curlew**, **oyster catcher**, **dunlin**, **redshank**, **sandpiper** and others, plus the **heron**, **mute** (on the southern part of the coast) and **whooper swans**, and **eider**, **teal**, **tufted duck**, **wigeon** and others.

In addition to these, the aerobatics of **ravens** are a feature of many cliff walks, particularly on Skye, while the **sea eagle** — quite recently reintroduced into Scotland on the island of Rum — might possibly be seen.

Conifer woodland (6,4,*14*,*15*). The commercial plantations provide cover for **rabbit, fox, wildcat, pine marten, roe deer** and others, but the trees are generally close together, thus keeping the sunlight from the forest floor and inhibiting the undergrowth necessary to sustain the smaller mammals and insects at the bottom of the food chain.

The bird life of the plantations can include **blue, great** and **coal tits, bullfinch** and **chaffinch**.

The Caledonian pine forest – a relic of the type of woodland which once covered much of the Highlands – is more open, and is comprised of Scots pine with a variety of broadleaved trees and a rich undergrowth of heather and berries. The few remaining areas of this woodland are now protected, and are often fenced off to encourage regeneration.

Broad-leaved woodland (7,8,*14*,*15*). The type of trees generally encountered are **birch, rowan, hazel, holly** and **alder**, with patches of **oak** on south-facing slopes.

ADVICE TO WALKERS

Always check the weather forecast before setting off on the longer walks and prepare yourself for the walk accordingly. Remember that an excess of sunshine – causing sunburn or dehydration – can be just as debilitating as snow or rain, and carry adequate cover for your body in all conditions when on the hills.

Snow cover on higher slopes often remains well into the summer and should be avoided by inexperienced walkers as it often covers hidden watercourses and other pitfalls which are likely to cause injury. Also soft snow is extremely gruelling to cross and can sap energy quickly. Walking on snow-covered hills should not be attempted without an ice axe and crampons.

The other weather-associated danger on the hills is the mist, which can appear very swiftly and cut visibility to a few yards. A map and compass should always be carried while on the higher hills.

Obviously these problems are unlikely to arise on the shorter, simpler routes, but it is always wise when out walking to anticipate the worst and to be ready for it. The extra equipment may never be needed, but it is worth taking anyway, just in case. Spare food, a first aid kit, a whistle and a torch with a spare battery should be carried on all hill walks. In addition, details of your route and expected time of return should be left with someone, who you should advise on your safe return.

From August onwards there is grouse shooting and deer stalking on the moors. If you are undertaking one of the hill routes, first check with the local estate or tourist office, thereby avoiding a nuisance for the sportsmen and possible danger to yourself.

COUNTRY CODE

All walkers, when leaving public roads to pass through farmland, forestry or moorland, should respect the interests of those whose livelihood depends on the land. Carelessness can easily cause damage. You are therefore urged to follow the Country Code:

Guard against all risk of fire.

Keep all dogs under proper control (especially during the lambing season – April and May).

Fasten all gates.

Keep to the paths across farmland.

Avoid damaging fences, hedges and walls.

Leave no litter.

Safeguard water supplies.

Protect wildlife, wild plants and trees.

Go carefully on country roads.

Respect the life of the countryside.

1 Neist Point

Length: 1¹/₂ miles (2.5km) there and back
Height climbed: 300ft (90m)
Grade: C
Public conveniences: None
Public transport: None

A short lineal route, undulating steeply, leading out to a lighthouse on an exposed cape. Clear paths and wonderful views of surrounding sea cliffs.

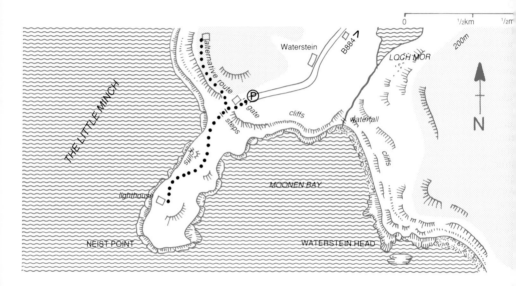

The Neist Point lighthouse is the most westerly on Skye, and it occupies a dramatic position on a narrow, grassy headland jutting out from a coastline of high cliffs. The short walk to the lighthouse is one of the pleasantest on the island.

To reach Neist Point, drive south from Dunvegan on the A863 for about a mile (1.5km), then turn right onto the B884. Follow this road (ignoring the numerous turns to right and left) for about nine miles (14.5km) until a road turns off to the left for Waterstein. Follow this for a little over two miles (3km) until the end of the road is reached. At this point there is a car park.

Go through the gate at the end of the car park and down the steep flight of steps beyond, leading down into the narrow neck of the headland. Looking to the left, there is a fine view of the tall

cliffs of Waterstein Head, with a dramatic waterfall cascading down the lower cliffs beyond, while ahead are the cliffs on the northern side of Neist Point. This is a splendid place for birdwatching, with fulmars, gannets and ravens all likely to be seen.

From the low neck the path climbs again, leaving the highest part of the headland to the right then drops back down towards the lighthouse – 62ft (19m), built in 1909 and now unmanned. Allow some time to explore the headland beyond the lighthouse, noting the fine views westwards to the Outer Isles, before returning by the same route.

From the car park there is an alternative, shorter route, out along the cliff-tops to the north. This walk provides a good view down to the lighthouse.

10

2 Coral Beaches

Length: 2 miles (3km)
Height climbed: Negligible
Grade: C
Public conveniences: None
Public transport: Bus service from Portree to
Dunvegan Castle

*A short lineal route through rough grazing
land and by a rocky foreshore, leading to a
fine shell and coral beach.*

The Coral Beaches are unusual in being composed
not of sand, but of a mixture of shell particles and
tiny pieces of calcified seaweed. This produces a
foreshore of a pale ochre colour, which turns to a
fine turquoise when seen through the water at high
tide.

To reach the beaches, drive to Dunvegan, then
turn north along the A850 for a mile (1.5km) to the
entrance to Dunvegan Castle: the seat of the Chiefs
of the MacLeods. Traditions dating parts of the
structure back to the 9th century are open to
question, but there is no doubt that the MacLeods
were in residence at least as early as the 14th
century. This makes Dunvegan the oldest castle in
Britain known to have been continuously inhabited
by the same family. It is now open to the public
and is well worth a visit while you are in the area.

Beyond the castle the road becomes single-
track and continues for another four miles (6.5km)
with Loch Dunvegan to the left. When the road
reaches a T-junction at Claigan (near its
conclusion), turn left, into a car park.

Walk through the gate at the far end of the car
park (please note: no dogs allowed) and continue
along the clear track beyond through an area of
rough grazing. Pass through another gate (noting
the sign warning about the bull) and continue along
the track, which now runs behind the shore. After a
short way a low ridge cuts across the route. Climb
over this and continue along the rough footpath
beyond to the Coral Beaches, backed by a pleasant
area of cropped grassland.

From the end of the headland, beyond the
beaches, there are fine views of the little islands of
Isay, Mingay and Clett, near the mouth of the loch,
and of the Waternish peninsula beyond.

Return by the same route.

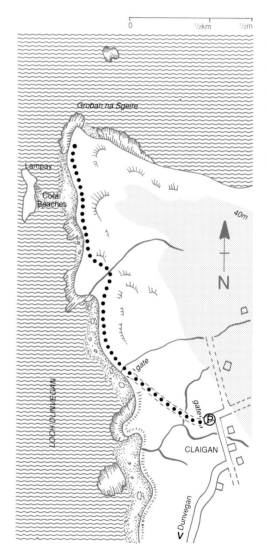

11

3 Waternish Point

Length: 8 miles (13km) there and back
Height climbed: Negligible
Grade: A
Public conveniences: None
Public transport: None

A clear lineal track through an area of rough grazing and moorland, leading to a ruined township. Fine views of coastal scenery.

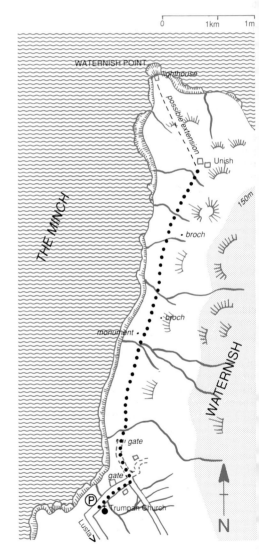

This walk starts at the car park opposite the ruin of Trumpan Church, near the end of the Waternish peninsula. The church seems a peaceful spot now, but in 1578 it was the scene of a notorious atrocity, when a party of MacDonalds from Uist barred the door and set fire to the roof thatch with the congregation still inside. The raiders themselves were subsequently killed by a vengeful party of MacLeods.

To reach the church, drive three miles (5km) north of Dunvegan on the A850, then turn left onto the B886 road. Follow this until it turns down to the shore at Lusta, at which point a single-track road cuts right. Follow this for a further four miles (6.5km), ignoring the roads cutting off to the right, until the church is reached on a low hill overlooking the Minch.

From the car park, walk on along a straight section of road. When this turns right at a right angle, turn left, through a gate and on along a clear track (no dogs allowed, please note). Follow this track through a field, through another gate, then on across an area of rough grazing and moorland. The track is good and the route is never in doubt.

Apart from the tremendous views westwards, across the Minch to the Outer Isles, there are a number of points of interest along the way. The first is a monument, to the left of the track, commemorating Roderick MacLeod of Unish, who died hereabouts in battle with the MacDonalds of Trotternish in around 1530. A short distance beyond, to the right of the track, is the first of two brochs (Iron Age defensive structures) visible from the route. The second is a little under a mile (1.5km) further on. At the end of the track there are a number of ruins, including one of a substantial two storey house. Beyond these, an extra walk of two miles (3km) (there and back) leads to the lighthouse on Waternish Point.

4 Waternish Loop

Length: 4-5 miles (6.5-8km)
Height climbed: 250ft (70m), undulating
Grade: B
Public conveniences: None
Public transport: Post bus service from Dunvegan to Gillen

A circuit on clear tracks and quiet public roads, through grazing land, moorland and conifer forestry. Fine views of coastal scenery.

To reach the Waternish peninsula, drive three miles (5km) north of Dunvegan on the A850, then turn left onto the B886. Follow this for four miles (6.5km) until it begins to turn down to the waterfront just beyond Lusta. At this point take the unnumbered road which cuts off to the right.

After a short distance the road enters a narrow band of woodland above Waternish House. One end of this route starts to the right of the road at this point, from a wide gateway beside a burn. If there is room to park by the side of this gateway; if it is not possible to do this without blocking the entrance then carry on until a convenient spot presents itself. If you are doing the whole circuit it is unimportant where you park, but if you are only doing the hill track, continue until the road for Gillen cuts off to the right. Follow this until it reaches a T-junction then turn right again. There is room to park at the end of the road.

Starting from the gate above Waternish House, walk up the clear track beyond, with grassland to either side. As the track climbs, the views to the south, of the islands and headlands around the mouth of Loch Dunvegan, begin to open up.

Continue along the track, by the left-hand edge of a stand of conifers (ignoring a track which cuts off to the right), then through the trees for a short distance before emerging on the far side of the hill. There are fine views ahead of Loch Snizort and the little Ascrib Islands, with the peninsula of Trotternish beyond.

A short distance beyond the trees the track splits. The right-hand track leads down to the shore of Loch Losait, while the left-hand track leads to the road end at Gillen. From this point either return by the same route or else follow the quiet public road back to the start.

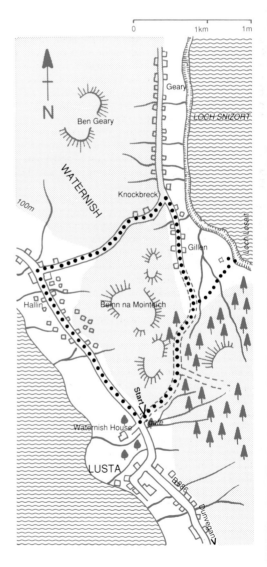

5 Quiraing

Length: 4 miles (6.5km)
Height climbed: 950ft (290m)
Grade: A
Public conveniences: None
Public transport: None

A series of rough paths through an area of soaring cliffs and extraordinary rock formations. Tough going in places but extremely dramatic.

Quiraing (Norse for the 'Ridge of the Fold') provides one of the most dramatic areas of geological formations to be found in Skye – rivalled only by the Old Man of Storr *(20)*, about 11 miles (18km) south along the ridge of Trotternish. To reach it, drive some 19 miles (30km) north of Portree on the A855. From Brogaig, just north of Staffin, turn left on to the single-track road to Uig. Follow this for around two and a half miles (4km) and, just after the road has zig-zagged up the face of the ridge, park in the car park to the left of the road.

Start walking opposite the car park, and follow a rough but clear track which runs along the base of the cliffs, with a steep grassy slope dropping down to the right, and isolated rocky hills emerging from the grass on the far side of a rough valley. The most imposing of these is The Prison: a huge, tilted square block. Level with the northern end of this block, a shaft of rock about 120ft (40m) high, called The Needle, rises amongst the towering cliffs to the left of the path. (A rough scramble up the narrow gully to the left of this leads up to The Table: a patch of flat grassland high amongst the imposing buttresses of the cliffs. This detour adds to the distances shown above.)

Continue along the path beneath the foot of the cliffs: past a small lochan to the right and through a gap in a stone dyke, noting the knot of peaks and ridges visible ahead. When the ridge to the left reaches its lowest point, climb up on to it, then turn left again, back along the top of the cliffs (taking all due care). The initial climb up the slopes of Meall na Suiramach is gruelling, but the views (including a spectacular one down onto The Table from above) are magnificent.

After a little over a mile (1.5km) the car park becomes visible ahead.

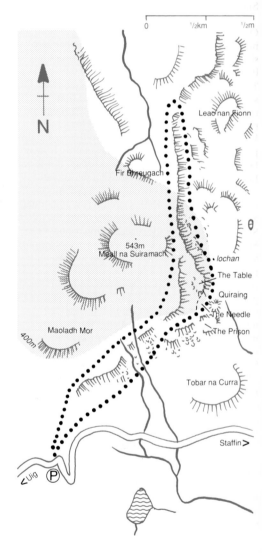

14

6 Old Man of Storr

Length: 3¹/₂ miles (5.5km)
Height climbed: 1000ft (300m)
Grade: B
Public conveniences: None
Public transport: Bus service between Portree and Staffin

A short, steep climb on rough tracks to an area of extraordinary and precipitous rock formations. Wonderful scenery; some care and sure-footedness required.

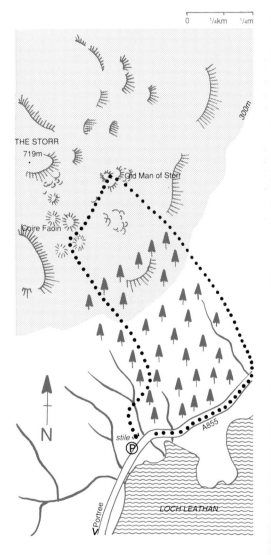

On an island rich in dramatic scenery, perhaps the most dramatic sight of all is the Old Man of Storr: a sheer pinnacle of rock, 160ft (49m) high, standing beneath the steep cliffs of The Storr (2360ft/719m). This famous geological curiosity is on the eastern side of the Trotternish peninsula, and can be reached by driving a little over six miles (9.5km) north from Portree on the A855 road for Staffin. Watch for the cliffs ahead and to the left, and park just before the start of a conifer plantation to the left of the road, near the northern end of Loch Leathan.

Cross a stile over the fence by the road, and walk up the slope beyond, with a dyke to the right and the plantation beyond that. The Old Man of Storr is visible ahead, with the buttresses of the Storr behind it, and a long line of cliffs sweeping away to the left. About half way up the edge of the plantation the path veers right, into the trees, and continues. It can be very wet under foot at this point.

Climb to the upper edge of the trees and look up the steep, grassy slope beyond. Beneath the massive cliffs there are two craggy protuberances like broken gateposts emerging from the grass. Start up the slope and aim to pass between them. The path is a steep one, but it is worth the effort, for once through the gap the route enters an area of extraordinary geological contortions. There are a number of paths beyond. Follow (carefully) whichever you prefer, through the cliffs and boulders, until the base of the Old Man is reached.

From this point there are splendid views across the Sound of Raasay, and south to the hills of southern Skye. The plantation is visible below, with a clear path running down to its left-hand edge. Follow this down to the road, then turn right to return to the start.

7 Portree Loop

Length: 2½ miles (4km)
Height climbed: 400ft (120m)
Grade: B
Public conveniences: Portree
Public transport: Numerous bus services to Portree

A short loop on rough paths (which can be damp in places) through grazing land and woodland and along a rocky foreshore. Fine coastal scenery.

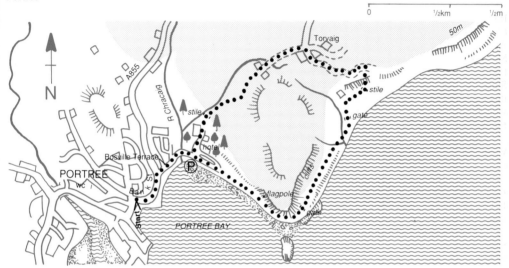

Portree is the administrative centre for Skye: a small, tight knit town clustered about a sheltered bay. The name means 'King's Harbour' – a reference to a visit paid to the island by King James V in 1540 – although the town itself was not developed until the 19th century.

This route leads out around the headland to the north of the bay, and starts from the town centre. Walk north up Bank Street, then turn right along the curving Bosville Terrace, from where there are fine views down into the busy anchorage. Keep right at the next two junctions, swinging east along the northern shore of the bay. Just after passing a parking area to the right, there is a split: the road heading off ahead left, the path (signposted 'jetty') continuing by the bay.

The path is quite clear at this point, and remains so as far as the viewpoint and flagpole (commemorating the association of the Nicolson clan with the area), but becomes rougher beyond, as it swings round the steep headland.

Just beyond the point there is a gate in a dyke. Go through this and continue across damp grassland, with a fence to the right, until another fence crosses the way. Turn left along this until a gate is reached; go through this and continue around the edge of the field beyond. At the top of the field there is a stile. Cross this and climb up the slope beyond before turning left along a clear track, climbing to the top of the hill.

When the track reaches the houses at Torvaig, take the track beyond the house to the left, heading down towards two large farm buildings. Pass between these and then continue across rough moorland, with Portree visible in the valley ahead.

Cross a stile as the path enters an area of woodland, then continue downhill, passing to the right of a hotel, before rejoining the original road near the car park.

8 Hallaig

Length: 5 miles (8 km)
Height climbed: Up to 800ft (250m), undulating
Grade: A/B
Public conveniences: None
Public transport: Ferry service to Raasay from Skye

A fine route on tracks and footpaths of varying quality, passing through areas of woodland, grazing land and moorland, and leading to a deserted township. Excellent views.

Raasay is a narrow island, running some 15 miles (24km) north to south and lying between Skye and Applecross on the mainland. It is reached from Skye by a ferry running from Sconser – three miles (5km) east of Sligachan – to the pier at East Suisnish. Please note that the distances shown for this route assume the use of a car (though a bicycle would provide more pleasure on these quiet roads) for the four miles (6.5km) to the start of the route.

Turn left from the pier as far as Inverarish, where a road cuts off to the right. Follow this, and at the next junction turn right again and follow the road across the moor to its conclusion at North Fearns. There is space for parking just before the last house on the road, beyond which a clear track continues.

Follow the track along the face of a wooded slope, with fine views across to Applecross and the islands of the Inner Sound. The track soon emerges from the wood and then continues, with the cliffs of Beinn na Leac up to the left, to a turning point above the little headland of Rubha na Leac. At this point there is a memorial cairn to 'the people of Hallaig and other crofting townships' (who were cleared from the land during the last century), and a splendid view opens up of the steep, straight slopes of the eastern coast of the island. Also, in the nearer foreground, there is a fine waterfall where the Hallaig Burn drops over a low cliff into the sea.

Beyond the headland the path gradually deteriorates and finally disappears by the Hallaig Burn. Cross the burn and climb up the slope beyond to visit the deserted township. From this point, either return by the same route or follow the burn up to its watershed and there join the rough path by the side of Beinn na Leac. This path eventually disappears, but not before the public road appears below. Turn left along this to return to the start; right to return to the pier.

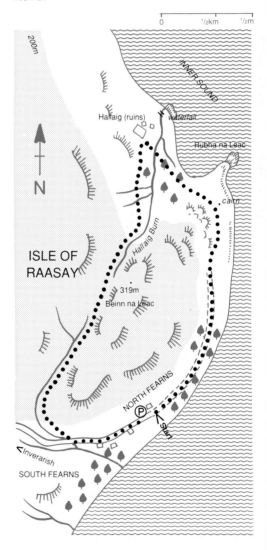

17

9 Point of Sleat

Length: 4-5¹/₂ miles (6.5-9km)
Height climbed: Undulating
Grade: B
Public conveniences: None
Public transport: None

A clear, lineal track through hummocky moorland leading to a tiny, rocky harbour, and to the lighthouse beyond. Fine moorland and coastal scenery.

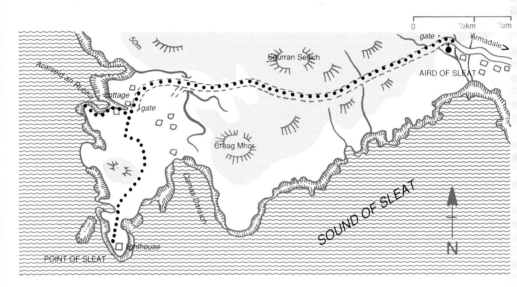

The peninsula of Sleat forms the most southerly part of the island of Skye, with the narrow Sound of Sleat separating it from Knoydart on the mainland to the east. Its scenery is somewhat gentler than that found in most of the island. It boasts, in addition, the pleasant little harbour of Isle Oronsay, and the Museum of the Isles at the Clan Donald Centre, Armadale House (once home to Lord MacDonald: descendant of the old line of MacDonald Lords of the Isles); well worth a visit while you are in the area.

This pleasant lineal walk leads down towards the Point of Sleat. To reach the start, drive south from Broadford on the A851 to Armadale. When the road swings left, down to the ferry pier, carry straight on for about five miles (8km), following the winding single-track road to its conclusion at the small church at Aird of Sleat. Parking is very limited here, and it may be necessary to drive a

short distance back along the road to find somewhere suitable (ie, where you are not blocking the roadside gates and passing places).

Go through the gate at the end of the road and follow the clear track beyond as it meanders through an area of heather moorland, with views over the surrounding sea opening up from the higher sections of the track. Shortly after crossing a bridge over a burn, the track splits. Keep to the right and continue, down to a gate by a cottage. Immediately beyond this, a rough track cuts left, leading a little over half a mile (1km) to the lighthouse on the point.

Alternatively, carry straight on after the gate, down to the tiny natural harbour. A short scramble over the rocks beyond, out to the point to the left of the harbour, provides a fine view southwards to the islands of Eigg and Rum.

Return by the same route.

10 Elgol

Length: Up to 9 miles (14.5km)
Height climbed: Undulating; 650ft (200m) on long return route
Grade: A/B
Public conveniences: Elgol
Public transport: Post bus service from Broadford

A long circuit on rough footpaths and quiet public roads. Some care needed in places, but matchless views of the dramatic Cuillin Hills on clear days.

To reach the start of this route, drive 14 miles (23km) south of Broadford on the winding B8083, which ends at the little settlement of Elgol on the slopes above Loch Scavaig, near the end of the Strathaird peninsula. As the road drops down towards the shore, look for the car park on the right-hand side.

To start the route, walk back up the road for a short distance, then turn left along a track (initially tarmac) behind some houses, signposted for 'Gàrsbheinn'. By the last of the houses there is a sign for a footpath to Coruisk. Follow this.

The rough path starts along a steep, grassy slope, with wonderful views (even from the earliest sections of the route) across Loch Scavaig to the island of Soay and the craggy peaks of the Cuillins. Beneath Ben Cleat the slope becomes even steeper, and sufferers from vertigo may not wish to follow the path any further. For the rest, continue across the foot of Glen Scaladal (crossing the burn can prove difficult when it is in spate, but it can usually be achieved dryshod), then on along the path beyond beneath Beinn Leacach to the bay at Camasunary, with its grassy hinterland overshadowed by the huge buttresses of Sgurr na stri and Blà Bheinn.

From this point, the shortest return is by the same route. Alternatively, look for the clear track which winds up the right-hand side of Abhainn nan Leac and over the hills to the east. The track runs for a little under three miles (5km) before joining the B8083, climbing to around 650ft (200m) at its highest point. Turn right along the road (generally quiet) for about three and a half miles (5.5km) to return to Elgol.

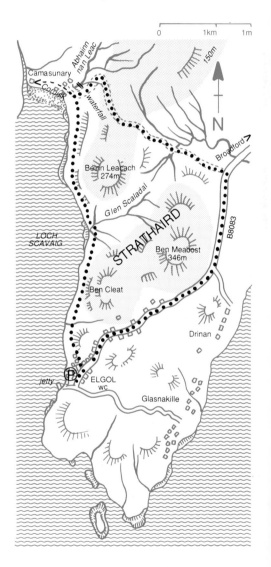

11 Glenbrittle

Length: 6 miles (9.5km) there and back
Height climbed: Undulating
Grade: A
Public conveniences: Camp site
Public transport: None

A long, lineal route on rough paths across rugged grazing land. Some navigation required when paths peter out at far end of route. Fine coastal scenery.

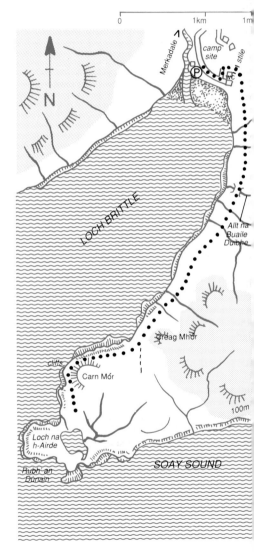

Glen Brittle curves around the western edge of the Cuillin Hills, and the car park at the point where the river empties into Loch Brittle is a favoured starting point for many of the routes through this dramatic range. These routes require some climbing experience, however, and none are described in this guide (those who are interested in the hill routes can obtain details locally). It is not necessary to take to the hills in order to find good walking, however, and there is a very pleasant coastal route running southwards from the car park towards the headland of Rubh' an Dùnain.

To reach the start of the route, drive west from Sligachan on the A863. After six miles (9.5km) the B8009 cuts off to the left. Follow this for about two miles (3km) to Merkadale, then turn left again on the unnumbered road for Glenbrittle. After about eight miles (13km) the road reaches the camp site at the head of Loch Brittle. Park in the spaces by the road and walk on into the camp site. Look for the public conveniences to the right of the road and walk down to the left of them, then cross the stile over the fence beyond. Two paths head off to the right – they run parallel, so either will do.

Continue along the slope above the loch. The ground can be very wet, and some agility may be required to cross the various burns which flow down the slope towards Loch Brittle, but the largest of these (Allt na Buaile Duibhe) does have a bridge across it.

After two and a half miles (4km) the path climbs up and around the shoulder of Creag Mhòr. From this point there are views of the islands of Rum and Canna, while the rough path can be seen to split in the low ground beyond the hill. Either path will lead on down to Loch na h-Airde, but the right-hand route, along the cliff edge beneath Carn Mòr, is drier, clearer and more dramatic.

12 Talisker

Length: 5¹/₂ miles (9km)
Height climbed: 400ft (120m), undulating
Grade: B
Public conveniences: None
Public transport: Bus service between Portree and Fiskavaig

A pleasant route on clear tracks; through rough grazing land at first and leading to a wide bay flanked by sea cliffs.

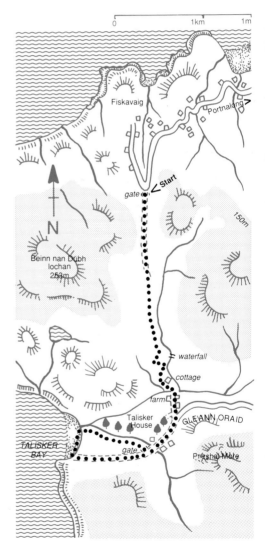

To reach the start of this route, drive five miles (8km) west of Sligachan on the A863, then turn left on the B8009. From Portnalong, turn left onto the road signposted for Fiskavaig. Some three miles (5km) along this road there is a severe hairpin bend. Look for a space to park here (being careful not to block any gateways).

Go through the gate by the hairpin and start walking along the track beyond; leading southwards through the rough grazing land of a shallow valley, with peat cuttings down to the left of the track. As the track continues, the rocky mass of Preshal More – looking a little like the half-eroded Sphinx in the Valley of the Kings – becomes clearer on the far side of Gleann Oraid.

After a little over a mile (1.5km) the track zig-zags down into the valley beside a waterfall. At the foot of the slope there is a cottage. Pass to the right of this and continue along the clear track beyond; through a farm and on to a metalled road. Two roads cut off to the right. Ignore the right-hand one (a private entrance to Talisker House) and take the other; with a steep slope to the left and a wall to the right with deciduous woodland beyond.

The track passes Talisker House and crosses a burn, immediately beyond which there is a sign to the right, indicating the 'scenic walk to the sea', and a gate. Go through this and follow a clear path by the side of the burn, flanked by trees and meadows full of wild flowers, down to the stony beach at the head of Talisker Bay. From here there are fine views of the great sea-cliffs to the north and south. Note the splendid waterfall cascading down the cliffs to the north of the bay.

Turn left along the shore to join a clear track which leads back up to Talisker House, then return by the original route.

13 Oronsay

Length: 3 miles (5km) there and back
Height climbed: Up to 250ft (70m), undulating
Grade: C
Public conveniences: None
Public transport: None

A short, lineal route through rough grazing land to a small, grassy island (cut off at high tide). Paths can be wet, but fine sea cliffs and coastal scenery.

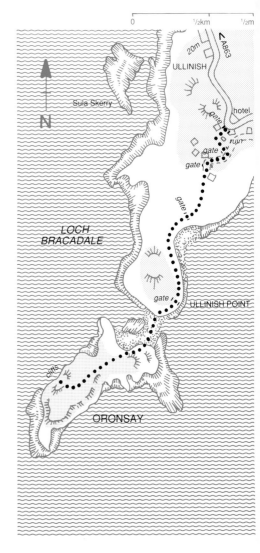

The name 'Oronsay' – quite common in the Scottish islands – is of Norse origin, and means 'tidal island'. This particular Oronsay remaining true to its name, **it is important to check the state of the tide before crossing.** The tidal section of the route is only short, and the island itself small enough to be crossed in a few minutes, but there is no point in risking becoming cut off.

To reach the route, drive nine miles (15km) south of Dunvegan on the A863, then turn right on the single-track road signposted for Ullinish. After a little under two miles (3km), park near the hotel. Go through a gate between the buildings opposite the hotel and follow the path beyond until the remains of a building appear to the left. Turn left, across an open area, to a small gate leading on to a metalled road. Turn right and follow this until a gate is reached to the right of the road, just before the last house.

Go through the gate and continue along a clear track. When a bay comes in from the left there is a second gate, beyond which the path becomes narrower, and can be very damp, but remains clear. Follow this to a further gate, near the end of the headland, beyond which the rough path drops down through a gully to the causeway of loose stones leading across to the island.

There are no buildings on the island, but the cropped grass provides pleasant walking, and there are dramatic cliffs around the western end. To get the best views around Loch Bracadale, climb up to the highest point (being careful when approaching the summit as the cliffs drop sheer immediately beyond). To the west is Wiay, and the smaller Harlosh and Tarner Islands, with Idrigill Point and Macleod's Maidens beyond. To the east is the lighthouse on Ardtreck Point, at the mouth of Loch Harport, while to the south the cottages of Fiskavaig are visible above the low cliffs *(12)*.

14 Plockton Loop

Length: Up to 7 miles (11km)
Height climbed: 600ft (180m)
Grade: B/C
Public conveniences: Plockton
Public transport: Post bus service from Kyle of Lochalsh

A possible circuit, starting on a clear footpath by the shore and continuing through a variety of types of woodland and farmland. Clear tracks and quiet public roads.

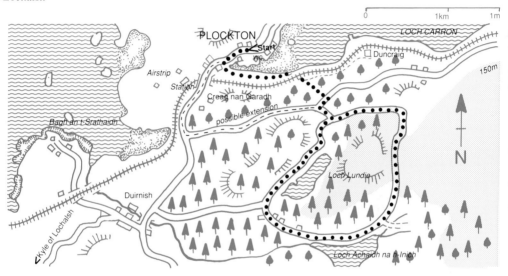

The little village of Plockton is just over five miles (8km) north of Kyle of Lochalsh along minor roads. It is one of the pleasantest settlements on the coast: a couple of streets of small houses and hotels spread along the edge of a shallow, well-protected anchorage. Looking north from the bay there is a fine view of the islands and rocky, wooded headlands around the mouth of Loch Carron, with the dramatic mountain scenery of Wester Ross visible beyond.

For this route, walk south from the centre of the village. When the bay ends to the left, there is a signpost for a footpath to Duncraig. Turn left onto this and follow it around the head of the bay, and then on between the railway line and the shore. There are fine views of the village and its anchorage from this stretch of path.

After a short way the path ducks under the railway line and starts to climb the wooded hill behind. A path cuts off to the left (to Duncraig); ignore this and carry on, climbing gently through the trees to join a quiet public road.

Turn right along the road to reach a junction. For a short route, turn right and follow the public road two and a half miles (4km) back to Plockton. For a longer walk, turn left, then left again at the next junction, and follow a narrow road through mixed woodland in a loop of a little under four miles (6.5km). Keep to the right at each junction, passing Loch Achaidh na h-Inich and Loch Lundie along the way; pleasantly situated amongst tree-covered hills. Be careful to shut the forestry gates behind you.

When the loop is complete, return either by the original path or by the alternative route along the public road previously mentioned.

23

15 Balmacara Forest Walk

Length: 2-4 miles (3-6.5km)
Height climbed: 400ft (120m)
Grade: B
Public conveniences: None
Public transport: None

Two fine forest walks on clear, signposted paths; passing through both conifer and broad-leaved woodland, and providing excellent views (particularly from the longer route).

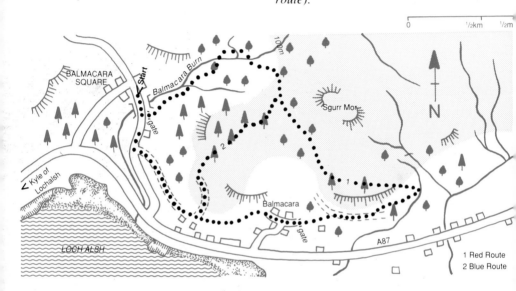

1 Red Route
2 Blue Route

These two routes start from the little village of Balmacara Square, in a valley to the north of Loch Alsh. To reach it, drive three miles (5km) east of Kyle of Lochalsh on the A87, then turn left onto a minor road.

Park in the village then walk south on the eastern exit road. After a short distance the road crosses the Balmacara Burn, and just beyond this there is a gate to the left signposted for the 'forest walk'. Follow this path along the burn side, with the slopes of Sgurr Mor visible ahead, until it enters the conifer plantation and begins a steep ascent. Once the climb has levelled out the path crosses the burn, then recrosses it, before climbing up to join a clear track. Turn right along this.

After a short distance a smaller path cuts off from the main track (just before it enters an area of beech woodland). For the shorter (blue) route,

continue down the main track; for the longer (red) route take the higher path, leading on along the slope of the hill, the trees gradually clearing to allow wonderful views of Loch Alsh, the narrow sound of Kyle Rhea and the surrounding hills of Skye and the mainland.

The path continues round the hill until it reaches a burn flowing down the slope through an area of oakwood, at which point it drops down to join a clear track. Turn right and at the first junction keep to the left (there is a post indicating the route). Shortly after this a gate is reached, beyond which a road continues in front of a house. Continue to the next house, then join a rougher path which continues through an area of gorse. At the next junction (at which the shorter route rejoins) carry straight on, back to the public road. Turn right to return to Balmacara Square.